Turn On Your
Psychic Powers

TURN ON YOUR

PSYCHIC POWERS

TARA SUTPHEN CHT

From
Sorce Moon Press

https://www.moonsorce.com

Sessions | Seminars | Products

First Edition: April 2026

Tara Sutphen

ISBN: 979-8-234-02487-9

To William, Hunter, Cheyenne
& Everest

I Love You... Forever

Acknowledgements

Thank you My Beloved Family & Friends

My Mother: Marianne Corey-Cramer

My Children: William (Karissa) Sutphen, Hunter Sutphen, Cheyenne Van Zutphen-Charleux (Alex)

My GrandAngel: Everest Sutphen

My Siblings: Scott Alexander-McKean (Sherri), Jason D. McKean (Sumire), and Amy McKean-Beaver

My Nieces:
Brionna Beaver (Jake & gr. Nephew Briggs), Shannon Beaver, Audrey Beaver

My Tribe: Marla Maples, Carmen Anderson, Lindi Holland, Marie Lehman, RC Matheson, Jules Bonny, Christopher Wilkinson, Will Tae & Carrie Smith, Jacquie Jordan, Patty Raymond, Linda McKean, Patti Stanger, Marek & Alina Girski, Swil Kanim & Lori Marshall, Kaitlin Robinson, Tiffany Trump-Boulos & Michael Boulos, Kristen Anderson, Michele Clark, Helen & Dale Fredericks, Stacy Christopher, Cynthia Hudson, Ann Slichter, Liz Young, Lena Jolton, Katie Clement Nelly Hart, Lyuba Ross, Jack McKeown, Matthew Engel, Randy & Dana Aldridge, Gerry Hagerty, Dr Mark Plotkin, Michelle Toms, Stephen Hall, David Jacks, Kathy Watson, Cliff Chatlien Davidson, Chris & Elena Starbuck, Dr Mark Hestrin, Walker Marchal & Ellis, Shail & Simmi Gulhati, Mahan Kirn, Sheri Shay Johnson, Carey Odom, Ron & Laiza Graziotti, Dawn Krug, Robert Hacker, Denise & Christian Charleux, Candi Cane Cooper, Paul Wagner & Kellianne Murphy-Wagner

Those Deceased who inspire me:

Jess Stearn, Treesa Robinson, Barbara May, Helene' Kayal, Kahlil Gibran, Anandamayi Ma, Baba Ji, Siddha Gurus, Ramses II, Alan Watts, Robert Friedman, Richard McKean, Robert & Lynnette Fusaro, BJ & Gloria Thomas, Jim Morrison, Shri Raman, Patrick J. Smith, Richard B. Matheson, Guru Dev, Entity Doctors of Casa Ignacio Abadania, Brazil, Abenda

I Love You all…

Table of Contents

Foreward

I wrote this book to help you study, prepare, and learn psychic awareness. Available to anyone willing to practice. I want to teach you how to recognize your abilities from wishful thinking. To translate subtle insight and practical skills for guidance every day. To retune your body to become awakened to your senses.

When I first started exploring my own sensitivity to distinct signs and messages, I didn't know yet what I didn't know. So I decided to start attuning to my psychic abilities. I began like you are doing now… you don't know where you are going, but it will be an amazing journey!

So I began exploring the supernatural realm. Even though, I had a psychic gift, I didn't know how to control it. I would blurt things out, and I really chastised myself for not being more tactful at times.

Your psychic attunement awaits you. What are you waiting for! Turn on your psychic powers. No more dead-end places, dead-end friends, dead-end relationships, dead-end jobs, or dead-end health regimes. Start making the right decisions and trusting your progress. You have a life to live and to live it well. It's time for your psychic powers to be turned on.

Tara Sutphen CHt

Introduction

Amid mystic realms are rare teachers candling the way with golden flame.

Seers of the unseen.

Muses and mentors who discern not fear, but blessings.

Not ends, but beginnings....not darkness but light.

In "Turn on Your Psychic Powers," the gifted and soulful Tara Sutphen has written a map to the wondrous.

Its many stellar chapters, of glorious invocation, guide us into the seemingly impossible; helping us understand not only prismatic intricacies of the psychic and paranormal, but how to recognize, embrace and master them....a distillation of the profound; rich with perceptions borne of her lifetime in divine terrains; a shaman and healer; renewing deceased spirits, lost faith.

Our extraordinary, inner potentials and selves far exceed the obvious; awaiting expression.

Sublime release.

In this prodigious volume, Tara Sutphen hands us the keys to our dormant marvels, writing with depth, wit and eloquence.

Whether you start in the middle, end or beginning, the book is addictive magic.

R.C. Matheson

"I rely far more on gut instinct than researching huge amounts of statistics." - Richard Branson

1
Psychic Ability

You may have gotten a lot of "psychic hits" during your life, where you say to yourself "wish I would've spoken up" or "I knew this or that before it happened". But day to day, you don't seem to have a clear connection to your intuitive ability, so you secretly wait for the next big "ah-ha" moment. And when it happens again. You're just as baffled. How did I do it? Why can't I control it?

Everyone is born to be psychic, but very few know how to use it. Although many mothers have "eyes in the back of their head". Oh yeah, that's when we know there are some ultra-psychic parents with tingling-spidey senses. Some teachers speak their "hunches" at school too. Knowing just what everyone in the class is thinking and planning, But they don't usually call it psychic ability, they may not call it anything. They just have "inner knowing".

When we begin to develop our intuition, we need to keep an open mind as we search for fragments of truth. Many doctrines and philosophies study humans before birth and after death. If you are taking the time to journal your impressions, you are creating a road map to see if you're on the right track.

Maybe it's time for you to read your "own" motivations and useful instinctive skills. We want to know we're going in the best possible direction. Also, that time and our mistakes aren't cheating us. We'd like to stop making errors and certainly live our purpose.

To start adding some clarity to your psychic ability. You can analyze how best you can learn to use your senses, as not everyone is impressionable in the same way. While some of you are more visual than auditory, or more feeling than have the sense of knowing. Some of you are seers through symbols or shamanic clues. This book is about opening your pre-thoughts and plans for review. We came to earth to live the best possible life. We want great health, fantastic love, a successful career, and an overall happy life. Are we succeeding in doing so?

Every stumbling block, can be used as a stepping stone. Do you check in with your intuitive or divination skill. You have keys to knowledge of unlocking your heart, and mind, and creating a connection with the divine. This book aims to guide you towards recognizing and harnessing your innate intuitive abilities, so you can navigate life with confidence.

Your inner sight

Intuition is often described as a gut feeling or a whisper in the back of the mind, but it is so much more than that. It is an unexplainable understanding that transcends rational thought. We will explore the essence of intuition, discussing how it manifests in daily life and the signs that indicate your intuitive senses are awakening. You will learn to trust your instincts and recognize the subtle nudges that guide you toward your true path.

Every individual has a unique way of perceiving intuitive information. Some may see vivid images, while others might hear specific phrases or experience strong emotions. We will delve into the various forms of intuition—visual, auditory, kinesthetic, and symbolic. By understanding your predominant intuitive style, you will be better equipped to interpret the messages being sent to you. You will also discover exercises designed to refine your abilities, such as meditation, dream journaling, and mindfulness practices.

Your inner compass

As you embark on this journey of self-discovery, it is essential to cultivate a deeper awareness of your thoughts and feelings. The importance of self-reflection and mindfulness in developing your psychic abilities. You will learn about grounding techniques, how to create a sacred space for contemplation, and the significance of maintaining a balanced emotional state. By tuning into your inner compass, you can navigate life with greater intention and purpose. While overcoming doubts and fears.

Many individuals struggle with self-doubt and skepticism when it comes to their intuitive abilities. We will address common fears that can hinder your progress, such as the fear of being wrong or the fear of judgment from others. You will learn strategies to overcome these obstacles, empowering you to embrace your gifts with confidence. Through personal anecdotes and testimonials from others who have walked this path, you will find encouragement and inspiration to trust your intuition and integrating intuition into your daily life.

Developing your psychic abilities isn't just about having those "ah-ha" moments; it is about integrating this knowledge into every day. We will work on harnessing practical tips on your decision-making process. You will discover how to ask the right questions, and listen for guidance. With practice, you will learn to recognize the signs and synchronicities.

Many ask if anyone can be psychic, and the answer is yes. There are a few individuals who possess an ability to perceive information beyond the normal sensory capabilities.

While I believe anyone can develop psychic abilities with practice and openness. The belief in psychic abilities varies widely among cultures and individuals, and many see it as a personal journey.

Some signs of psychic ability

Intuitive Insights: You can have strong feelings or hunches about people or situations that can turn out to be accurate. This might manifest as a sudden understanding of a person's emotions or motives without them saying anything.

Intensified Sensitivity: You may feel over-whelmed or introverted in crowded places or experience strong emotional reactions to the people or the energy around you. This sensitivity can also extend to physical sensations, such as feeling someone else's pain or discomfort.

Dreams with Messages: Your dreams may include vivid imagery or scenarios that later manifest in reality. You might find that you frequently have prophetic dreams or dreams that convey important information about your life or others.

Premonitions: You sense events before they happen, whether it's knowing a friend will call or predicting an upcoming occurrence or event. These premonitions can be minor or significant changes or messages.

Synchronicities: You notice frequent coincidences, such as repeatedly encountering numbers, meetings with others or symbols in various contexts, leading you to believe a deeper message is at play.

Empathic Abilities: You can easily pick up on the feelings of others, often without them expressing it verbally. This ability to empathize deeply can lead to emotional exhaustion if not managed properly.

Interest in the Occult or Spirituality: You find yourself drawn to topics such as tarot, astrology, or meditation, and you may feel a natural inclination to explore these areas, suggesting a deeper connection to the spiritual realm.

Feeling "Different": You might have a persistent sense of being different from others, feeling like you do not quite fit in, which can stem from your unique perceptions and experiences that others may not share.

Visions and Clairvoyance: You may experience flashes of insight or mental images that provide clarity about a situation or person. These visions can come spontaneously and often feel like they carry significant meaning.

Communication with Spirits: Some individuals may report experiencing connections with spirits, whether through seeing, hearing, or sensing their presence, leading to feelings of guidance or messages from the other side.

Each of these signs suggests a connection to intuitive or psychic abilities, but recognizing them may vary from person to person. And you may have many untapped ways of exploring your potential.

A woman raised her hand at a seminar to ask why she wasn't getting much from the psychic exercises I was teaching from the stage. I asked her, "tell me how you are perceiving?" She started to share what her visions were, and I told her she connects to answers being symbolic. Much like how you would interpret a dream.

All of you will be better at one modality over the other. It's just finding and exploring what you are naturally inclined toward and to practice being good at it.

How to begin:

To begin developing your psychic abilities, focus on daily meditation and mindfulness. Keep a journal and/or recording your experiences. You'll have a record of your hits and misses. This helps you clarify your potential. Don't worry if you're not a detailed journal writer, just provide yourself a few sentences on how you perceived a question, or exercise.

How to Breathe:

Breathe in peace and exhale chaos... a few times, coming into a relaxed state of being. Then I want you to breathe in beauty and exhale blessings and beauty to others, breathe in money and exhale blessings of prosperity to others, breathe in health and exhale blessings of health to others, breathe in love and blessings of love to others. You want to breathe in prosperity in all ways... and exhale prosperity and relaxation, being open to your psychic ability and all the possibilities of living a great life.

Open your hands to attain the beauty and bounty of the earth.

We ask it, we beseech it, we mark it and so it is…

Note: You can add a prayer here.

Your Prayer:

2

Opening the Psychic Senses

Here are a few suggestions to reflect on as you start exploring your psychic ability.

Practical guidance:

Clarify your intention
Develop mindfulness
Be present
Meditate 2 min, 5 min, 15 min daily
Guided meditation
Focus on your breath
Journal your experiences
Practice listening to yourself
Practice empathy
Use structured exercises
Be grounded
Be polite
Be aware of your environment
Raise your vibration

"Your pain is the breaking of the shell that encloses your understanding." - Kahlil Gibran

3
Asking the Right Questions

Here are practical tips to start asking some questions. Remember, you're going to be keeping a log or recording of everything you ask.

- Be clear-cut, not unclear
- Ask for 1–2 outcomes
- Do you want to know facts or assumptions
- What are your risks
- Ask one question at a time
- Ask a deadline or timeframe
- You can ask follow-up questions
- Ask a clarifying question
- Clarifying a goal
- Breaking down a problem
- Exploring options
- What are 5 approaches to goal
- What are the pros what are cons
- what's stopping you from pursuing ___

- What are the potential risks of pursuing
- What are the consequences
- What's one thing I'm overlooking
- What would make my intuition wrong

Your Notes:

4
The Clairs

What incredible skill would you like to learn first? A professional psychic tunes into our past, present, and future. How are they picking up this information on us. Are they sensing, feeling, or seeing aspects of our personal and professional life. How are they perceiving who I am.

The Clairs:

Clairvoyant - Clear sight and visions through their mind.

Clairsentient - Clear feeling and tuning in to feel your feelings.

Clairaudient - Clear hearing and audible messages from their higher self, your higher self, their spirit guides or angels.

Claircognizant - Clear knowing - gut feelings and inner and outer knowing.

Clairgustance - clear tasting - on the tongue, food or drink

Clairalience - Clear smelling - through the nose, smelling scents, perfumes and nostalgic smells

Clairtangency - Clear perception - awareness, mental impressions

Listen to yourself and others as they give their greatest clue on where they need to start developing their instincts. Remarks such as "I hear ya", "yes, I see", "I know" or "ya know", "I feel for you" — Identifying in some way gives you clues on what is your and others' strongest clair.

Note: if you are getting bad thoughts or feelings. Raise your vibration and say some prayers. Psychic ability is to gain clear and practical advice, not create instability or chaos.

How to raise your vibration:

Close your eyes. You are sitting, touching the floor or the earth with your feet. Breathing deeply and exhaling. Listen for the sound of the earth (scientifically the earth makes a sound) allow your own sound to resonate with the earth's sound. Whether it is a hum, ring, buzz or vibration. You hear it on the surface of the earth or in middle earth. Match your sound to the earths sound… it may take a few moments. Remember your sound to the earths sound. Peace will then wash over you.

You are now in resonance with the earths energy. You are no longer fighting or fidgeting, you are flowing in peacefulness.

"Life is really simple, but we insist on making it complicated." - Confucius

Clear Intuition

Clairvoyant - Clairsentient - Clairaudient - Claircognizant - Clairgustance - Clairalience - Clairtangency

We all long to have the inner guidance to make great decisions! Intuition is the ability to understand something immediately without the need for rationalization. Learning to re-use our instincts to help us maneuver our lives rather than human conditioning and second-guessing ourselves. It's a gut reaction, you're not overthinking.

How do we get to that part of ourselves again? Sometimes it's saying yes to invitations. Calming nerves, so you can listen to your inner voice. Cultivating your body compass and somatic awareness; if you get an uncomfortable physical impression then you know the answer. Whether you listen to yourself will be the test. Write down your hunches. Remember that fearfulness isn't always the compass, it's knowing how to create a solution or making a decision.

A large part of this is creating Sentience, being cognizant of feelings and sensations, not requiring knowledge or mental stimulation but acting assured its the right answer or choice. It can refer to the depth of awareness an individual possesses about oneself and others.

The most familiar four psychic abilities are clairvoyance (sight), clairsentience (feelings), clairaudience (hearing), and claircognizance (inner-knowing). Start to recognize which sense is your strongest. Align to your values. Breathe deeply and practice meditation.

There is a fine line between reality and illusion. Psychic ability can be learned, but it takes diligence and practice. There are many different intuitive ways to become proficient.

Let's begin to develop some different ways to recognize your psychic ability(s). We will start with "the Clairs". I want you to remember to allow yourself to observe and be present with your new found abilities. Remembering that everyone carries their own upsets, problems, health ailments and issues. Everyone is fighting their own battles and they need to be consoled. People need your honor, charity, good will, unconditional love and integrity. There is a solution to all problems. The underlying psychic code is to soothe others and look for answers and solutions.

Your Notes:

Sight - Practice Visualization: Clairvoyant

When you begin to study your clairvoyance skills. Write down your daydreams. Focus on scenes and images in your minds eye. You can do some visual exercises. You see objects or actions as they have happened before, in the present, or before they happen, beyond the range of natural vision. You might have to practice this.

Clairvoyance is "clear sight", you're seeing in a different psychic way. This can take people by surprise when daydreams become a manifested event. Many times you can be 'wandering in your mind's-eye', wishful thinking or deep in your imagination when these observations come to you. Learning to control them is the next step.

When you answer someone who is asking you a question, and you say "I see", this often refers to your use of inner visualization. You might see who others need to know or you have special problem solving abilities; which you see on paper, people's general sense of purpose or direction or events happening before you. You can prefer to see things and not discuss them. Caught in the act of watching instead of reacting. Lucid dreams or vivid dreams. You have probably been shut down by others when you expressed your sightings. You could write them down and keep a journal.

Signs you are Clairvoyant, you see:

- Auras

- Energy fields

- Flashes of Light

- Mental movies

- Movement out of the corner of your eye

- Mists or Fog

- Colors

- Symbols

- Visions

- Puzzle pieces

- Dreams

- Goals

- Desires

- Events being played out

How to practice Clairvoyance:

Close your eyes and breath deeply a few times, with your eyes closed concentrate on your inner-sight. Feel your third eye tingling or being activated. Focus on an object or person.

Do you see an aura?

Connect to their third eye. What kind of information are you getting. Write or record your experience.

Your Notes:

Feelings - Practice Empathy - Clairsentience

Empathy is the ability to sense the feelings and emotions of others. Clairsentience means "clear-feeling", you being emotional, compassionate, and cognitive without taking it on as your own feelings. When you're opening psychic centers many times you can think you're emotional, sometimes you can feel or have peculiar thoughts, yet you could be picking up on the person sitting next or across from you. So with that in mind don't take on any sentiments of exhaustion or overt behavior. Try to not be confused or defensive. An example is, "You may ask someone if they are okay, and they may answer, they are fine: and many times you know something is wrong and clearly, they are not okay". You may need to learn to shield yourself

Center yourself:

To center yourself, rub your hands together and place them on your heart for a moment.

There is always a way to come back to yourself, your feelings, emotions, and balance. Not everyone is a psychic empath like you are, know when nurturing others soothes not only them but you as well and when to steer clear from people who will be energy sucklers.

Your non-visual, non-verbal cues of empathy can be deeply ingrained; you will say "I feel" this or that: when you have a guess or suspicion. When the tough get going, you are in the forefront. When you follow the cues of others, you can feel that person's pain, fear, or joy. You don't always know how you know, but you "feel or sense it". You are a deep-feeling person with strong emotions and can be very loyal. You may want to write down your feelings and hunches in a journal.

Signs you are clairsentient, you feel:

- Sensitive to people around you
- Sensitive to your environment
- Sensitive to nature and animals
- Sensitive to energies around you

- Must recharge with quiet time
- Goosebumps or Tingles
- Sense others intentions
- You justify others bad manners
- Pick up moods, emotions and thoughts of others
- Your mood can change if someone else walks into a room
- You can be called too sensitive or even dramatic
- Crowds can be too much for you or your tired when out among people

How to practice Clairsentience:

Close your eyes and breathe deeply a few times, with your eyes closed concentrate on your inner-feelings. Feel your solar plexus tingling or being activated. Focus on an object or person.

Do you see an aura?

Connect to their solar plexus. You might begin to see movies of an object or a persons feelings and their journeys. What kind of information are you getting. Write or record your experience.

Hearing - Practice Deeper Understanding - Clairaudience

This is perceived on a sagacious level. Messages in clairaudience mean clear-hearing. Many people say "I hear you" when they overhear the nuances of any conversation. Generally, they can be easily tuned into the news, music, gossip, the next tables conversations, external noise and others moods. They usually are curious about all the sounds around them,

Though spirit content can be external, its either coming from a source outside of yourself, or it's an internal voice in your mind. It can be a few cue words or you can be clued in to listening to a full conversation. That can be tricky to remember though as messages usually are important. Sometimes you hear voices of past loved ones, or sounds that trigger a message. Voices that give you an audible message; maybe even in your dream state, a whole conversation to remember. However you might be having these audient messages, you will tune in on a deeper level and discern what needs to be heard. Reaching a deeper understanding or gain news. Usually this is to provide guidance and sound advice, it can be a warning before something is about to happen - Good or Bad.

If you're getting unnecessary chatter or a lot of negativity though, close your eyes, take a deep breath, put both your hands on your solar plexus and say out loud "I raise my vibrational energy". Remember clicking back into our LifeForce energy and the God Light is very easy.

Signs you are ClairAudient, you hear:

- You hear your name being called
- You hear the radio or songs in the distance
- You hear people chattering and no one is there
- You hear words in the distance
- You hear distinct words from people

- You are inspired by words
- You know someone from their voice
- You can decipher peoples voice patterns
- You can hear illness or pain in the way people talk
- You hear conversations in your dreams
- You hear warnings in someone else voice in your head
- You have conversations with others in your daydreams
- You hear clear advice
- You can commune with animals and nature

How to practice Clairsaudience:

Close your eyes and breathe deeply a few times, with your eyes closed concentrate on your inner-hearing. Connect to your ears tingling or being activated. Focus on an object or person.

Do you see an aura?

What are you hearing of an object or a persons feelings, sensations, plans and their journeys.

What kind of information are you getting. Write or record your experience.

Inner-Knowing - Practice Intuition - Claircognizance

Your intuition is very high when you have the inner knowing or gut feeling. A lot of times claircognizant people say "I know". You can "fly by the seat of your pants" in any situation, you instinctually know what to do. There is a "right-ness" and you follow it. Claircognizance is an intuitive ability of clear-knowing. You're not in the wavy gravy of feelings, you subconsciously and instinctively move proactively.

You are inclined to trust yourself. You may not know why you know but you feel the urge that it's the correct manner to say or do. It's usually quick and effortless. You know when things aren't right and all the things that could go wrong. But if you're feeling a positive surge, you are tapping into your higher consciousness. You can experience clear thoughts, and decision making and feel a deep sense of well-being. Constructive Instinct is powerful to embrace, you become nimble and easy as opposed to doubt. Some people are too brisk, some people ponder too long — try to be instinctual and tap into your inner knowing.

Signs you are Claircognizant, you have a knowing:

- I just know somehow
- Flash of insight
- Flash of inspiration
- Pick up skills quickly
- React quickly
- Make decisions of safety
- You have innate knowledge on a subject

How to practice Claircognizance:

Close your eyes and breath deeply a few times, with your eyes closed concentrate on your inner-knowing. Connect to your gut-knowing, your animal instincts. You might not see or hear the messages, but you innately "know". Focus on an object or person.

Do you see an aura?

Are they fidgeting or calm?

What gut reaction are you sensing with an object or a person motives, sensations, plans and their journeys. What kind of information are you getting. Write or record your experience.

Your Notes:

Clear tasting - on the tongue, food/ drink - Clairgustance

Clairgustance refers to an ESP (extrasensory perception) where some one has the ability to perceive taste without the presence of food or drink. This phenomenon allows a person to experience tastes through psychic means, associated with intuitive insights, Past life recall or spiritual experiences.

- Intuitive tasting
- Flavor associations
- Sensing Dish ingredients
- Taste emotions
- Cultural tastes
- Symbolic tasting
- Energy tasting
- Healing tasting
- Illness tasting
- Past Life tasting
- Metals tasting
- Elemental tasting
- Smoky tasting
- Parched and dry

- Alcohol tasting
- Telepathic tasting

How to practice Clairgustance:

Close your eyes and breath deeply a few times, with your eyes closed concentrate on your inner-tastebuds. Connect to your stomach and mind being activated. Focus on an object or person.

Do you see an aura?

Are they fidgeting or calm?

Are you satiated or hungry?

Are you feeling ones animal instincts in connection to food.

What are you empathically picking up of an object or a person with their motives, sensations, plans and their journeys around food/drink/ or anything to do with something in the mouth or tongue. What kind

of information are you getting. Write or record
your experience.

Your Notes:

Clear Smelling - Nasal Scents, nostalgia - Clairalience

Clairalience refers to the ESP to perceive scents or odors without the physical presence of a source. This phenomenon allows individuals to experience smells associated with spiritual insights, memories, or even the emotions and states of others.

- Health detection scent
- Emotional detection scent
- Memory trigger
- Environment smell
- Spiritual aromas
- Elemental scents
- Past life scents
- Symbolic smelling
- Perfumes
- Odors

How to practice Claircognizance:

Close your eyes and breathe deeply a few times, with your eyes closed concentrate on your inner-smelling. Connect to your nose and mind being activated. Focus on an object or person.

Do you see an aura?

How is it making you feel to smell these aromas and odors of an object, place or a person. Be open to smell sensations, and plans.What kind of information are you getting. Write or record your experience.

Your Notes:

Clear Perception - awareness/ impressions - Clairtangency

Clairangency refers to the perception of sensations or feelings through touch/contact, with the ability to read impressions and information about people, objects, things, or situations. This circumstance allows for one to receive intuitive insights by touching or being near to something or someone, leading to heightened awareness and understanding.

Each clairangency experience can show connection between touch and psychic perceiving .

- Tactile Intuition
- Object reading
- Energetic transfer
- Healing touch
- Textured touch
- Physical sensation
- Past Life touch
- Telepathic touch

- Elemental touch
- Symbolic touch

How to practice Clairtangency:

Close your eyes and breath deeply a few times, with your eyes closed concentrate on your inner-touch. Connect to your heart and hands being activated. Focus on an object or person.

Do you see an aura?

Are they fidgeting or calm?

What other Clair is coming into play?

Are you able to see or hear messages. What are you aware of in touching an object or a person. How are you getting your perceptions Whether it be their motives, sensations, plans and their journeys. What kind of information are you getting. Write or record your experience.

Your Notes:

5
Practitioner Titles

When learning to use your intuitive abilities, many often use divination methods and modalities. These are considered analytic, observational, and mystical.

Here's a list of practices of yesteryear and today.

Alchemist - Base metal to Gold, Seeking the Elixir of Life

Augurer - Soothsayer

Charmer - Fascinating & Pleasing

Clairvoyant - a Seer

Conjurer - conjures spirits & Sorceress/ Sorcerer

Diviner - supreme being or Theologian

Enchanter - Delights & Fascinates
Fortune-Teller - predicts the future
Magician - Illusion Producer & wizard
Medium - Speaker to the Dead
Seer/Seeress - Speaks of Future Events
Shaman - negotiator between natural & supernatural
Sorceress/Sorcerer -
Thaumaturge - Worker of Wonders & Miracles
Warlock - male witch
Witch - Wicca & Modern Witchcraft
Astrologer - Study of the Heavenly bodies and human affairs
Bear Walker - Walker between the Worlds
Channeller - Medium & Speaks to the Dead
Crystal Ball Gazer/ Scryer - observe images through crystal ball
Forecaster - predicts weather; contrives & plans
Oracle - Medium of Wise Counsel
Palmistry - Reads hands & palm
Psychic - Reads the human soul or mind: supernatural
Predictor - advance special knowledge
Harbinger - Omen & Signs for future event
Herald - Messenger

Prognosticator - forecaster & predictor

Horoscopist - Casting of Horoscopes

Sibyl - Women as Oracles

Telepath / Telepathist - Mind reader

Spiritualist - the Dead communicates to a Medium

Tarot Reader - Predictor of 78 playing cards

Archimage - Great Wizard, Magician or Enchanter

Medicine Man / Woman - Possess Healing & Supernatural powers

Spellbinder - captivates through powerful speaking

Theurgist - Supernatural System by Egyptian Platonists

What do you want your title or titles to be:

"Nothing is impossible, the word itself says, 'I'm possible!" -Audrey Hepburn

6
Psychic Experiments

Besides the writings, throughout the book I'm adding some psychic experiments for you to try. So you can start to open your intuition. We all have it, but at an early age we start to lose it and settle in with the gravitational pull and our earth life. We forget we are from somewhere else. And me, like you; really try and live in the here and now. But with my early life changing events, I had the opportunity to involve myself with the other world and when I started to explore, a new world opened up for me. Since the invitation was open, I would revisit a lot and established a solid relationship with my spirit guide, Abenda. Over the years I had a very hard time sharing stories about me, but I will convey a few here in this book. So you get to know me a little better, Abenda a little better and the

Famous Writers. Many of you already know them, and by reading their books. They were wonderful writers.

You may not want to speak to the dead, but I'll give you some information on how to stimulate your psychic ability. Many times its easier to start with some small experiments to see what is your strongest sense.

When you begin to practice to be psychic, you'll learn things about your self, such as what is your compelling sense. Then you begin to take your strongest senses deeper and gain more understanding about yourself and others. The more you learn to be psychic, the easier you'll know how to use your intuition and psychic abilities. There are numerous fun ways to test yourself and your friends. Developing through exercises and games can be enjoyable, as well as useful. Remember to keep a log and journal of all your activities and observations. That way you'll be able to go back and double check your "triumphs".

Future Prediction:

This can be precognition and clairvoyance. Or maybe you receive the information in another way.

Predict:

- Whose on the phone before answering

- Whose going to call you that day

- Winning sports teams

- News Stories

- Political outcomes

- Historical outcomes

- Weather outcomes

- What will my activities be on the weekend"

7

Precognition

Visions, dreams and different divination tools can stimulate your insights and psychic ability. Predictions are potential outcomes. You can get a tingle, hunch or a flash. Sometimes it's more empathically related, you can feel elated and excited, or these feelings can go the other way too of dread or fear. Or maybe in your head, you are seeing or hearing something good or bad.

It is important to know, when you are communicating these precognitive thoughts, it is wise to do so in a polite manner. Whether it is predictions for yourself, others, the environment or the world. This book is to help you understand your personal process or guide you into creating your own approach and method.

You may only have erratic hunches but with some practice you begin to learn a system that gives you some control on your psychic abilities. You may not want to have a career as a psychic. But having these abilities will help you in every choice and decision you can make. It's best to record or journal your findings as we want to clear with ourselves and others as much as possible.

Your Notes:

8

Aura Reading

Squint your eyes and examine someone's energy around them, with practice you begin to see a glowing color or hue. The more you practice, the easier it will be to see the auras of people, animals, trees and plants.

White / Light
strong life force, charitable qualities, resonance

Blue
connection, ideas, creativity

Green
Love, balance, health

Yellow
communication, clarity, productivity

Red
ardent, passion, moods

Pink
friendliness, playful, sentimental

Purple
wise, mystery, compassionate

Indigo
Intuitive, instinctive, understanding

Orange
Energy, attention, bravado, vitality

Teal / Turquoise
Modern, refreshing, healing

Gray / Neutral
shy, subtle, disorder (health or lifestyle)

Silver
bonded (otherside/earthly), fellowship,
divine purpose

Gold
privileged, advantage, inventive

Your Notes:

9

Telepathy

Telepathy is easy to practice with another person. Picture in your mind - a color, word, shape, symbol, object, and see if the other person picks it up in symbology or manifest reality. Switch and see if you can pick up images and their thoughts.

You may be really excited to play with telepathy on everyone you know, but be sensitive and polite to others feelings and boundaries.

Telepathy, defined as the direct transference of thoughts or feelings from one person to another. It has intrigued humankind through the centuries. Its origination can be traced back to ancient times, and cultures, primarily the Greeks, Egyptians, and East Indians. The Great Greek Philosophers, such as Plato and Aristotle formed theories on thought and perception, and delved deeply in their studies of the mind.

Spiritualism was on the rise in the late 19th century. Telepathy began to gain attention as well as the exploration of the mind with telepathy. Trailblazers Sigmund Freud and Carl Jung investigated theories related to the unconscious and conscious mind

Practicing Telepathy:

To develop telepathic abilities, one must begin with a few foundational practices. First, cultivate a strong sense of intuition. This can be achieved through meditation, hypnosis, mindfulness, and self-reflection, which help to quiet the mind and sharpen one's awareness.

I'd use the Clairvoyance technique. As practicing visualization techniques can also help in developing telepathy.

Close your eyes and breathe deeply a few times, with your eyes closed concentrate on your inner-sight. Feel your third eye tingling or being activated. Focus on an object or person.

Do you see an aura:

Connect to their mind with your mind. What kind of information are you getting. Write or record your experience

Your Notes:

10
Hypnosis and Psychic Ability

As Many of you know I'm a Clinical Hypnotherapist as well. With my Hypnosis skills mixed with my Psychic Ability, I like to help others strengthen their minds and open to the possibility of Great Health, Prosperity, Love, Happiness and Success. I have found this to be very fulfilling work.

Hypnosis is often depicted as a mysterious and almost magical process, one that can unlock hidden potentials within the mind. The concept of attaining psychic abilities through hypnosis intertwines with various beliefs and practices, suggesting that the subconscious can be accessed and harnessed to reveal extraordinary insights and capabilities.

The process of hypnosis involves guiding an individual into a deeply relaxed state, where the conscious mind recedes, allowing the subconscious to surface. In this state, individuals may experience heightened awareness and openness, potentially facilitating access to intuitive knowledge or psychic phenomena. Many practitioners believe that through hypnosis, one can tap into deeper layers of consciousness, where latent psychic abilities lie dormant.

For some, hypnosis serves as a tool for exploration, enabling them to discover their innate gifts or abilities, such as clairvoyance, telepathy, or precognition. As the individual delves deeper into their subconscious, they may receive images, feelings, or messages that suggest a connection to a greater universal knowledge. This can lead to profound realizations and the development of psychic skills, as the barriers between the conscious and subconscious mind begin to dissolve.

However, the relationship between hypnosis and psychic abilities is subjective and often varies from person to person. While some individuals may experience significant enhancements in their intuitive capabilities.

The pathway of hypnosis as a means to attain psychic ability is rich with potential, often colored by personal experiences and beliefs. Whether viewed as a legitimate practice or a fascinating exploration of the mind's capabilities, it invites individuals to journey within themselves, seeking to unlock the untapped reservoirs of power and attainability that lie within.

In my meditations I sometimes visualize metaphorically "a psychic box", this is an ethereal vessel where I ask questions and seek "in my mind" an item that will symbolically give me an answer. In exploring your perception, reach into a box to retrieve a meaningful object to your question. The *psychic box is empty and waiting for you to retrieve an object in your meditation's inner vision.

I have a recording called "The Path Meditation", it "directs your inner eyes" down a path to explore symbolic representations of your career, relationships, health, and spirituality. Everything you experience on your meditative walk can provide metaphorical clues.

Sunny weather, as you stroll to a house representing your relationship; would be considered a positive indicator. As opposed to "If it was a sleet storm" which might be considered worrisome. Experiencing an easy or difficult-path gives clues on your sub-conscious and conscious choices you're making in real life.

When you're working with intuition, our minds don't know what is illusion -vs- reality. Through our *nine senses, we are conscious of the world around us and consider it real. We have a validity of what we see with our eyes and touch with our hands. Everything looks genuine, therefore we don't really question any of it. Our nine senses are at work through our bodily involvement. We hear, smell and encounter hot and cold. These are earthly facts. We don't imagine pain if we hurt ourselves. Yet Eastern philosophies say that the world is an illusion. Without the mind and our nine senses, this world does not exist. We can create change with our viewpoint and ideas to generate the human experience, but there are gaps, when we are sleeping and in meditation.

After we wake up from sleep, or when we get out of deep meditation and return to ordinary awareness, we feel that there was an intermission in our consciousness, in which the outer humanity hardly existed for us. There was no world for us at that time. I am not saying that the world ceased to exist at these moments, it halted to exist for us, for our consciousness and awareness of it. Our lives occur when the nine senses and mind are in cohesion.

I take this concept to mind through my research with brain-mind programming and even when I was writing the book "Soul Writers". I'm a firm believer in working with the subconscious understanding while using hypnosis, sorcing, shamanism, mysticism and intention.

There is no real difference other than *prayers are communications with the divine and asking God many different things, where *sorcing you are praying for a direct outcome on said person, place or thing. It's just more directive. We have different ways of perceiving our psychic abilities.

Let's look at "sentient mind" - it is the depth of awareness you have for yourself. At most cognitive levels, sentience can be conceptualized as 'your identity' or self-recognition and contains metacognition which is your ability to think and reflect upon one's own thoughts. It's the capacity to have feelings.

Senses are the physiological process of interpretation. There isn't an agreement or consensus among neurologists on what constitutes a sense. One of the definitions state, sense is a natural faculty where we recognize external stimuli. The established senses are sight, hearing, touch, smell and taste. However the research says we have nine different senses and at least two other senses in organisms. Debates about the number of senses arise typically considering the categorization of the various cell types and their mapping regions of the brain. Nine senses are the nine levels of consciousness, which consist of sight, hearing, touch, smell, taste, feelings, identity, memory, and energetic drive.

Nine senses are the nine levels of consciousness, which consist of sight, hearing, touch, smell, taste, feelings, identity, memory, and energetic drive.

prayers are communications with the divine and asking God many different things, including protection

sorcing you are praying for a direct outcome on said person, place or thing

Your Notes:

What are your fears:

Here are a list of fears:

Fears can be instinctual, learned, or situational. Here are some broad categories and examples:

heights
snakes
spiders
loud noises
darkness
Fear of judgment
 public speaking
 rejection
failure
Not meeting standards
death
meaninglessness
uncertainty
anxiety
panic attacks
phobias
lying
germs
medical procedures

loss of control
harm to self or loved ones
social judgments
Uncertainty

We can recognize our weaknesses in hypnosis, and look for a root cause. Learning to be more confident in our psychic abilities to help strengthen our resolve.

"Live in the sunshine, swim the sea, drink the wild air."
-Ralph Waldo Emerson

11
The Box

I started gathering objects, photos and sayings to put in an actual *real-life box. I collected items to represent accomplishing some of my personal goals. I chose a "Golden Buddha Chest" made in Thailand for my *God Box. Every day in my prayers and meditation time; I would have the box on my lap. I would ask for God's Blessings.

I would also drink Ho'oponapona water from a blue bottle. A Hawaiian tradition called Blue Solar Water. It is a simple, homemade, energized water intended to cleanse, purify, and heal your body and mind.

I generally thought I was sorcing and praying for the inside contents of the box. But to my surprise… Six months later, I was standing before one of the largest golden Buddha's of the entire world. Incredible; if my jaw could've dropped to the floor it would have! I couldn't believe I stood before this magnificence.

Big Buddha Temple is in Ko Samui, Thailand and sits impressively on a small rocky island. The local name is Wat Phra Yai, its golden, 12-metre/ 39 foot seated Buddha statue was built in 1972. The Big Buddha sits in the Mara posture, with the left hand palm up resting on the lap and the right hand facing down, the fingers hanging over the knee and grazing the ground. It depicts a time during Buddha's journey to enlightenment where he successfully subdued the temptations and dangers thrust at him by the devil-figure Mara by meditating and remaining calm. The pose is a symbol of steadfastness, purity and enlightenment. I counseled with one of the monks, they pray and talk with you of your questions, issues or problems. The monk tied a string bracelet on my wrist.

You would think... I just booked a ticket to go see a giant Buddha. But it didn't happen like that. I have a client-great friend, Patti Stanger who came for an appointment, and she announced she was going to do a birthday revolution. This is when your astrology is configured to a location for said year. Patti said, "it looks like I'm traveling to Asia". I chimed, "I'll go if your plans include praying in the Temples." A few weeks later we were flying off for Thailand and Hong Kong. We prayed all throughout magnificent temples. We had such an amazing time. So many magical experiences.

*God Box is a some kind of real box, you start gathering objects, photos and sayings to put in it, collecting items to represent accomplishing some of your personal goals.

*Real Life Box is the God Box, but I also use the Psychic Box in Meditation.

*psychic box is empty and waiting for you to retrieve an object in your meditation's inner vision.

"Seek spiritual riches within. What you are is much greater than anyone or anything else you have ever yearned for."
–Paramahansa Yogananda

12
How To Make A "Psychic Box"

Touching the wood face of the Golden Buddha Chest. I open to fill it with magazine cut-outs of houses, goals, sayings, money, oils, checks, love notes to my children, lists for my career, and as I finish my silent prayers with the box I include a technique where I allow the energy around my body to brighten and expand. I call this "sorcing".

In my hypnotherapy practice I'm always asking my clients to center themselves and to see and feel the angels/sentinels, who I regard as the guardians who guide and protect us individually on the earth. These are your spirit guide's helpers. It can be Archangels,

Shaman, Monks, Saints, Rabbis, Priests, Totem Animals, Mythical Creatures or whomever you want them to be. The Sentinels stand north, east, south and west surrounding you.

You may feel like you are making them up, but I've experienced magical miracle after another over the years as I try to penetrate the portal barriers and vibrational thresholds. For many years, I would quiet my mind in a hypnotic theta state and follow otherworldly routes to try and figure out the different spiritual or etheric levels of heaven and earth.

That is to say, I'm trying to capture an idea or theory of what humans are doing on the planet. Where we come from, basically, and where we'll go after we die. This can be subjective as there may be places for all Christians, and religious places. Such as: Valhalla for all Norsemen, the Great Buffalo Hunting Ground for Native American's and the list is long. It's all about thoughts are things, and our desires help with the creation process.

Having had the two NDE (near death experiences) I follow the internal map of where I've been, and being "there" enough times to convey some information back to you. My spirit guide Abenda has chosen high vibrational spirits to answer questions via Automatic Writing. I know it's hard to believe there is life besides our gravitational green covered Gaia. But in our subconscious mind, we know the universe is vast and there are so many unanswered questions. Remembering as we gaze in the night sky, stars are suns for possible other planets.

Mindful of not getting "too out there", I try to keep my counseling work centered on using earth energies, our ancestors, spirit guides and angel/sentinel helpers. The sentinel helpers work for everyone, we just have to ask them. Our soul journey is hard work, and it takes a village to raise us all into awareness, goodness, blessedness and continued goodwill.

When using "the Psychic Box" in my meditations. I go into a trance and ask a question, reach into a box metaphorically and bring out an object to answer the question.

Yes, you could even bring out an elephant, every object has a metaphorical meaning and would allow for some clarity to the issue at hand. I'm usually trying to trick consciousness through brain-mind programming to develop wellness or success. Shamanically deciphering what I can pull from this treasure chest, it can be the meaning of moon cycles, the stars, constellations, animals, trees, waters, formations, nature, weather, houses, rocks, food and inanimate objects. I use personology, somatotyping, mannerisms, speech, words and handwriting. Sometimes, I utilize Astrology: Eastern and Western types, and any divination system.

Your Notes:

The only person you are destined to become is the person you decide to be." - Ralph Waldo Emerson

13
Psychic Radar

I've written and recorded many meditations, and I've been nominated for spoken-word Grammy's. I began my psychic sciences journey by first learning Personology, then studying Palmistry, Handwriting Analysis, Hypnosis, Automatic Writing, Channeling, Astrology - Western and Eastern, Shamanism, Mysticism and... I'm always still learning. I was tutored by Jess Stearn, Helene Kayal and Barbara May for many years. Whenever I had questions they gladly helped me seek an answer.

I do shamanic or druidic exercises to gain clues or directions. My clientele work consistently with me on different subjects, many times they have exceeded their expectations of having exemplary lives. When you put a little elbow grease into your intentions, good surprises start to happen.

I studied under Helene Kayal, a French Moroccan Mystic and Barbara May, an incredible Shamanic Astrologer. I took classes and readings from them, always asking questions on theories or unusual formulations. I studied Christianity for the first twenty years of my life and have enough friends and scholars, to quantify other religions. I had my bookstore and I collected rare Occult books from all over the world. I figure we can't know everything about the subjects we love to study due to our duration of time on the planet. But I really want to think that I'm cramming in as much wisdom and mysterious knowledge as possible this life to add to my Akashic soul Records.

My first unusual experience seemed to happen when I asked my mother to use the same check out woman at our local grocery store. As a little four year old, I knew Sue needed my friendship. My mother who is quite empathic in her own right didn't really understand my choosing to talk to her. My mom, a full time nurse, had 3 kids at the time and our "great-great invalid Uncle lived with us, needless to say she was a little over-worked. Sue was in terrible emotional pain, and she would speak to me of her little boy while my mother was checking out groceries. I remember it, as though we were almost in a bubble as the atmosphere changed. Nobody was listening to her, but me. She wouldn't divulge much, but I knew he was sick and they were both struggling.

One day my mom got a phone call and Sue asked if "I could come over." When we got there, the coroners van was in the driveway. Her little boy had died, I walked into her house, she was sitting in a chair in the far corner of her living room. I sat by her and said softly to her, "the Angels are here". I knew the portal to the other world was open in the next room.

For me, all the walls were gone. There were many beautiful angels and they were taking the boy's spirit and ethereal body with them. The angels waved at me, and the boy looked back at me. I waved back, and then I looked at Sue.

I remember my mother going over and start to speaking "nurse" and asking questions. I remember being proud of how she was handling Sue and this situation.

I'd been having to help my father through his grief of losing his mother and his mental torment of partially blaming himself at that time also. I understood his level of anguish.

Even at that age, my first inclination was to call in the Archangels, who I call sentinels. Maybe that's why I have ended up living in the Los Angeles aka "the Angels" area for so long. I know so many wonderful helpers, Doctors, Practitioners, Psychics, Alternative Specialists, Human Angels and Shaman of the world.

A few years back… Marek, my Polish Shaman friend picked us up from the airport in Seattle, my mother and I were his passengers. My Mom interjects excitedly how she brought me home as a newborn to a nearby lake. I tell him, "the name of the lake was Angle, obviously not knowing how to spell before I was born. I wanted to come to Angel Lake". In his deep Polish accent, he says "of course you did Tara".

My Mom and Dad lived in Hollywood, California, where I was conceived. They were newlyweds but my Mom as an RN, decided to return to her homeland of Alaska to work at Native Hospital. On her 8th month, my parents met again in Seattle; half way from Alaska and California. I was born healthy, but I would need extensive medical care in the next months to come. At that time I had my first NDE (near death experience) having surgery for 7 1/2 hours and given last rites.

My memory is a dimly lit operating room with the surgeon begging me to stay for my sad Mother. What seemed to occur when I was a baby is after the surgery, I recollected all interaction. Over the years I find most children can't remember much until the age of 5. My memory includes babyhood, toddler-hood, motivations, feelings, overreactions, odd behaviors and problems of children and adults in my vicinity.

When I was a baby and would cry, I would be furious I couldn't talk yet. Motor skills couldn't happen soon enough. I felt the dog understood me more than the parents. Although they were trying hard to stay in love. My mother was unconditional and super in love, whereas, my dad was loving, but he was wrestling with himself and his choices.

He had been in World War ll and already had a failed marriage. My mother and his brothers were his greatest advocates during his life. And My maternal great grandparents (my mom's grandparents) lived near by when I was a baby and they were full of beaming overt gooey love as thick as honey. I really enjoyed them.

I could recall past lives. There is one thing I was clear on very early, I know why people don't recollect their past lives. Many of them are full of unfinished business or terrifying experiences. We'd all be anticipating an overblown event or over-reacting to people. It's easy to read the current programming of adults and their stress levels. Just think if they all knew about what they did, or what someone else did to them in a past life. They would fret all the time and make themselves more anxious. Instead being suppressed as it is with gravity, and it's probably the best thing for our nerves. I observed other kids weren't disturbed by much, even if they had more recall. In general, children remind us to recapture our innocence.

Have you experienced a past life?

14
Dreams

Dreaming is the transmission between our conscious mind and our unconscious mind; during the night, most people dream. It is called REM sleep. Whether you remember your dreams or not. Here are 5 types of dreams.

1. Night Dreams

Delta is deep sleep. Usually you can remember a dream about an hour and half at the end of your sleep time, sometimes you can only vaguely remember. You are still dreaming the rest of the hours in your sleep time, but that gets even more vague unless you are journalling.

There seems to be a coded subconscious form of communication and even symbology. Your dreams could be telling you many messages about your urges, desires, and/or memories. There can be hidden psychic messages about the future or spirits communicating with you.

Your dreams can also be in color or black and white. Usually when you awaken, you can shortly forget the dreams, so if you want to decipher them you must write them down right away. They usually hold a lot of messages if you want to recall and study them. Keep a journal and pen next to the bed.

2. Day Dreams

You are probably in alpha/beta going into theta waves. You could easily nap, but you are just deep within your mind. Daydreaming puts you into a theta state of mind. Theta is linked to meditation, visualization and light sleep. It's Probably the more anxious a person is, the less they relax and day dream. During the day the average person can daydream 70-120 minutes.

Its best if you stay in a positive mindset, solution oriented thoughts, thinking the best of yourself and others. Don't complain in your head, or heart. I

ts best if you try and stay in positive frame of mind so that you create positive and productive outcomes. These fantasies are about creating your own reality, and even though you can wish you'd said or did something differently. It's best to keep the discussions you're having with yourself upbeat. The moment we dip into a downward spiral, we can fall into depression, isolation, and defeat. These sentiments are easily generated, which can squelch our confidence.

Keep your imagination going in a good direction, the universe has recognition of your real life and of your subconscious imaginings. If you want a deep and clear mind, you have to encourage your daydreams to be positive. We have been given this life as a gift and we have to trust we can handle it the best possible way. And the first is daydreaming on what we want and why we want it, and that it is the best outcome for us.

Lucid Dreams

These are dreams when you are asleep in delta and begin to go back into theta, where you start to dream about real life, people who are dead or alive that you know, and their talking to you about real problems or issues, you are in a awakened - dreaming state of mind. Visitations in our dreams from our deceased relatives, family, pets or friends; or even a prominent person in your community or spiritual person can usually mean they come to impart some kind of message or advice. You can direct your dream, and even answer back but you know you are asleep. A lot of time this can be people giving you directions or even following them somewhere. You can look, feel, hear and smell authentically.

Concocted Dreams

Recurrent dreaming while you are in delta sleep state. Sometimes you think you're already awake, walking out the door or in a place you visit, sometimes you keep going to the same place. You can be driving, You can be going to school or work, only to find you are just waking up. Sometimes you dream over and over and then wake up. These dreams are probably trying to tell you something and journalling about them would be an excellent way to decipher what the message might be.

Nightmares

These can be downright scary dreams. You are fighting someone or something in your dream. And in your waking life you may be trying to work out your problems and issues; how you are seeing your nightmares can be a clue into seeing how you are handling your waking life. Hopefully in a calmer and more practical way than dreams can be. Nightmares are sometimes connected with sickness or stress. Trauma or drama could play a role in nightmares, also drugs and/or alcohol. When having a nightmare, you can awaken pretty shaken, this is when you write it in your journaling start to decipher.

Deja-vu

Déjà vu means "before sight" in French, and rêvé means "dream", this type of dream could be considered "precognition".

How To Analyze Your Dreams:

Some of us don't remember much when dreaming. Because you're usually having a full night of it or at least the last hour and half before you awaken.

Sleeping is essential to our well being. If you aren't dreaming at night. You might need to restrategize your sleep schedule. It's important to improve sleep by trying to get 7-9 hours of sleep. Create a relaxing, cool and darkened sleeping space.

The best way to remember dreams is to write them down as fast as you can. At night I also tap my forehead and remind myself, I'll remember my dreams.

Dreaming seems essential to our development and growth, there are no rules to follow. But it can tell us how we rest and recharge. There is a larger context of our individual self-discovery that we can dig deeper for the meaning behind the dreams. Journal your dreams; during the night or upon first awakening. Write a few words or sentences if you can't remember all of it. Don't worry, and if you haven't dreamt, add to the diary, "no dream" or if you had one and don't remember write that in the journal. Remember to write out your feelings related with the dream.

If you recently have a relative, friend or even a pet die. Don't take sleep aids, drugs or alcohol if you want a visitation. Everyone and your pets come to say "goodbye". If you start dreaming about them, they are there with you.

"The Intuitive Mind is a Sacred Gift." - Albert Einstein

15
Divination Modalities

Tarot
Astrology
Crystal readings
Psychic readings
Palmistry
Aura readings
Many More Modalities

I began working on the Alaska pipeline when I was 19 years old. We got paid to ride the jet to work… the best part. It was like we lived on the moon, I worked at the base operations camp in Prudhoe Bay. Living in the Arctic was oddly fascinating and we were a small village of people. One day a man named Sharva Venta, asked if I'd like my astrology chart. I gave him my birth information and he hand wrote in small writing a whole notebook, all about me. I still have it in my files. That was my first experience with astrology.

I still knew nothing of metaphysics when I met Jess Stearn years later. Jess was a huge author, many times on the "New York Best Seller" list, his favorite genre and research was metaphysical and paranormal subjects. I had no idea about any of it. But Jess knew, and he invited me to every seer, psychic and channeler to see what they would say about me.

I really didn't know about tarot or auras or any of it either… All I knew is I'd had 2 major NDE's and my life and the players in it, are never an accident. Jess and I would sit around afterwards and I'd give Jess psychic readings and he would give me some. He told me, I'd meet a man I'd marry through him. I did meet Dick Sutphen and got married on Jess' deck in Malibu. I also had a baby on Jess' birthday. He was at the hospital when Cheyenne was born.

When I got married, I was studying divination books in my spare time and my husband asked if I wanted to open a book store so that I could get any books I wanted. I named the store "Malibu Shaman". It is now owned by my stepson Scott Sutphen. But the years I owned it, I'd fly to New Mexico, Arizona and Utah to get Native American jewelry and gifts, go through all the publisher warehouses to buy books for the store and listen to lots of New Age music, we created a listening bar.

I first started studying Palmistry from a Cosmopolitan Magazine article. Little did I know that I would someday be writing for major women's magazines sharing divination articles. Numerology, Astrology, handwriting, palmistry and other modalities. I soon started learning handwriting analysis. I wanted to research if the hands had any connection to handwriting analysis. I realized not really, although both of these modalities are good to know. I continued with my personology analysis and began studying face and body types. I was friends with Bruce Vaughan, who wrote the book "Body Talk". It was at this time I decided I better start learning

Astrology. I knew it would be a huge endeavor, and many years of in-depth research, and it has been. I didn't just want to learn western astrology, I wanted the ancient teachings. I obtained an amazing teacher, Barbara May. We became best friends over the years. I only realized recently how Lois Rodden, the great astrologer studied my chart. I became proficient in western and eastern Astrology. I'm still passionate about learning. And through Astrology I learned mathematics and numbers are the true language of the universe.

As I immersed myself in astrology, I sometimes locked myself for days at a time in my cabin learning complex formulas. I looked for profound and difficult effects that the positions of celestial bodies at the time of one's birth can have on personality traits, life paths, and relationships. I became fascinated by how the interplay of various astrological components and math formulas, along with the sun, moon, and rising signs and aspects, could paint a comprehensive picture of an individual's character and experiences. Each chart I interpreted was like a unique fingerprint, revealing the potential and challenges we face in life.

My exploration didn't stop at astrology; I ventured into tarot reading, captivated by the rich symbolism and archetypes that the tarot cards offered. Each card told a story, resonating with universal themes of love, challenge, and transformation. I found joy in conducting readings for friends and clients, helping them navigate their current situations and encouraging them to embrace their journeys with confidence and clarity.

The more I learned, the more I realized that divination was not just about predicting the future or uncovering hidden truths; it was about empowerment and self-discovery. I sought to share this understanding through my writing, classes and seminars. I contributed articles to various women's magazines, offering insights into astrology, palmistry, and the metaphysical arts. I aimed to demystify these subjects for readers, helping them realize that they, too, could tap into their intuition and understand the energies surrounding them.

And in the early 1980's my husband and I would teach the psychic seminars in Sedona. The first of their kind, with developing the names and promoting and researching the vortex's. It was quite a little rustic town then, no real restaurants, just a cowboy kitchen and I was a strict vegetarian then. I could only get an iceberg salad, cowboy beans and green beans. No hotels either, just a few motels. The one movie theatre, the owner would walk up and down with a flash light to make sure you weren't putting your feet on the seats or littering. "Back in the old days of Sedona".

My connection with Jess Stearn, Dick Sutphen, the metaphysical authors, and New Age musical artists, and my store thrust me into a community of seers, psychics, and channelers. They sparked my curiosity to the vast universe of metaphysical knowledge. I was introduced to practices such as aura reading and crystal gazing, each adding another layer to my understanding of human energy and spiritual connection. I often reflect on my beginnings in Prudhoe Bay, where my journey had first been sparked, and how far I had come since those early days of working in the Arctic.

As I continued to develop my skills, I also delved into the study of numerology and Gemetria, recognizing the profound significance of numbers in our lives. I learned how numbers could reveal patterns and cycles, offering insights into personal development and life lessons. This mathematical foundation complemented my astrological studies beautifully, as I began to see the connections between numbers and celestial movements.

Throughout this journey, I remained deeply passionate about learning and evolving. I attended workshops, read extensively, and connected with like-minded individuals who shared my enthusiasm for metaphysics. Each encounter, whether with a wise teacher or a curious beginner, enriched my understanding and inspired me to delve deeper into the mysteries of these psychic sciences.

As the years have passed, I embrace the role of mentor and therapist to others who seek knowledge in astrology, divination, and metaphysical practices or just finding their way out of difficult events and situations. Hypnotherapy has designated my skills in guiding others on their paths, helping them uncover their potential and navigate the complexities of their lives.

The transformation from a novice in Prudhoe Bay, Alaska to a seasoned practitioner and writer in the metaphysical field was a testament to the power of curiosity, learning, and connection. Now, as I look back on my journey, I am filled with gratitude for the experiences that shaped me. From the small village in the Arctic to the vibrant community I built in Malibu and Los Angeles, every step along the way has contributed to a rich tapestry of understanding and wisdom. I continue to embrace the mysteries of the universe, ever eager to learn more and share my insights with all of you. My Odyssey is ongoing, and I remain excited about the possibilities that lie ahead in the realms of astrology, divination, and the metaphysical arts.

*Divination is an ancient practice that encompasses a variety of modalities used to gain insight, guidance, or knowledge from the spiritual realm or the universe. Each modality has its unique methods, tools, and traditions, appealing to different individuals based on their beliefs and preferences.

Your Notes:

Celtic Cross Layout

16
The Cards

Tarot cards, affirmation or oracle decks are a good way of testing telepathy; you can practice by yourself and write down what card you think you chose. First, center yourself and become quiet and centered, pick a card and connect to the card you've chosen. Don't be brash or lack patience with yourself, this is practiced divination. Sit in your deeper way of understanding and don't wildly guess. Then move on to predictions, take out your journal and record what you receive. In a few weeks go back and check. You may then get a glimpse or full view of your developmental psychic patterns.

What do you see in the card

Tarot cards and wisdom decks of all kinds are really fun. developing psychic awareness. You can try giving yourself simple readings, working with one question and one card at a time. Remember your question, in regard to the answer. You can also choose a general card for the day and see how the card applies to the outcome that day. Follow the interpretations in the pamphlet or guide book, remember to decipher and tell a story with the picture of the card and to close your eyes and get a feeling.

Tarot Card Reading: Tarot consists of a deck of 78 cards, each with distinctive imagery, and messages. Shuffle the cards and don't read upside down cards unless you turned them upside down. All cards are upright unless otherwise.

When I first started to learn Tarot I had a very small set of the rider-waite card set, and now I own probably 100 sets of tarot and oracle cards. I love to do tarot cards, and my favorite decks are Italian decks. They are "the medieval Scapini" and "Marchetti decks".

I have taught many people from my seminars beginning tarot. But who has mastered it the most is my brother Jason, who is now called "The Om Tarot Wizard" - Jason D. McKean. He is prolific in his list of career accomplishments; including being an amazing psychic tarot reader. He's been always behind the scenes producing this or that. He participated in a "4 day Psychic Boot Camp" with me and 4 others participants. I put them through the paces, early morning to late night. He was a wiz at tarot right away. Why I say Wiz, is because he looks like a wizard. He has a long beard and looks magical. And…he has a very nice manner, perfect for helping others. Not only does he have many books on learning Tarot now, he teaches classes and offers private sessions. He teaches for Japanese students with his Japanese interpreter. The Japanese students accompanied him to Egypt, Greece and Turkey. He's also the voice on many OM recordings, "Eternal OM" his voice has resonated to selling a million copies.

Tarot reading is a divination practice that uses a deck of tarot cards to gain insights, and guidance. Tarot can be originated in Europe during the 15th century. It emerged as a card game named "tarocchi." During the 18th century tarot cards became more esoteric in occult societies.

The tarot deck consists of 78 cards split into two sections, the Major Arcana and the Minor Arcana. The Major Arcana is 22 cards and the Minor Arcana which consist of 56 cards.

Tarot Deck

Major Arcana: The Major Arcana cards are "0 to 21" and portray powerful archetypes and all around common themes.

Minor Arcana: The Minor Arcana is divided into four suits, each representing various situations in life.

Cups: correlating with emotions, relationships, and intuition. The Cup cards indicate emotional connections.

Wands: correlating with action, progress, and ambition. The Wand cards indicate passion, inspiration, and personal growth.

Swords: correlating with ideas, thoughts, challenges, and conflict. The Sword cards indicate the mental realm, struggles, and decision-making.

Pentacles or Coins: Correlating with material aspects, work, and finances. The Pentacle cards indicate the manifestation of goals and the material world.

Each court card numbered Ace - Ten, and four court cards: Page, Knight, Queen, and King. The court cards can represent people or character traits in your reading.

To conduct a tarot reading:

Prepare Your Space: Find a quiet, comfortable space

Choose Your Deck: Select a tarot deck which resonates with you.

Shuffle the Cards: While you're shuffling, concentrate on your question or intention.

Single Card: A quick pick. A straightforward reading providing an immediate answer to your question.

Three Cards: this correlates with the past, present, and future relating to your question.

Then you have the **Celtic Cross layout:** 10 cards

Your Notes:

Write your reading in your Journal. Keeping a tarot journal can be helpful for tracking your readings. Write down the cards drawn, your interpretations, and any insights gained. This practice can help you develop your skills.

Tarot Reading

Practice Regularly: The more you practice, the more comfortable you will become with the cards and their meanings.

Ask Open-Ended Questions: When formulating questions, try to ask open-ended questions rather than yes/no questions. And I discourage repetitive questions. As you might want the outcome to be different than what appears on the cards for you.

Stay Unbiased: Approach readings with an open mind and remember you're having fun. Don't base your life or important decisions around readings. You're not to get frustrated, upset or angry. You are learning, continue to gain knowledge and use every reading toward a *"positive or hopeful"* outcome.

Be Patient: Be patient while you develop your skills..

I find Tarot reading to be enjoyable. And My brother Jason is "The Tarot Wizard". We actually are a whole family that loves to sit around and relax reading Tarot.

17
Astrology

Astrology: This modality involves the study of celestial bodies and their influence on human matters. Astrologers create natal charts based on the exact time, date, and location of a person's birth, deciphering the planets mathematical positions and the aspects to reveal personality characteristics, and possible life directions. Astrology provides a cosmic perspective on life's challenges and opportunities.

Astrology has fascinated humans for centuries, serving as a guide to understanding the universe's mapping system. Three prominent systems of astrology—Archaic Arkana Astrology, Western Astrology, and Eastern Vedic Astrology—offer unique perspectives and methodologies. Each system reflects different cultural viewpoints, historical backgrounds, and methods for interpreting celestial effects on human life. Understanding the differences among these systems can provide valuable insights into their respective approaches to astrology.

Archaic Arkana Astrology

Archaic Arkana Astrology is a lesser-known system that draws upon ancient wisdom and esoteric traditions. This astrology is associated with mystical teachings and celestial calculations that were once associated with Chaldea, Mesopotamia, Egypt, and Greece, and maybe even earlier with Lemuria, Atlantis, and Parts of Meso and South American observatories.

It has roots in Hellenistic astrology, which evolved from the earlier Babylonian and Egyptian systems. Alexander the Great, brought these Astrological archives out of Chaldea to Egypt.

In Archaic Arkana Astrology, the emphasis is on the spiritual and symbolic meanings of celestial events and old mathematic equations and formulas. I use a combination of astrological symbols, mythological stories, and archetypal imagery, old mathematics combined with new mathematics to interpret the influences of planets and stars. I know only a handful of Astrologers in the world who practice this way.

Western Astrology

Western Astrology, widely practiced in Europe and the Americas, is the newer Scientific mathematics. This system is calculated by the use of the tropical zodiac, which is based on the seasons and the position of the Sun in relation to the Earth. Western Astrology typically divides the zodiac into twelve signs, each corresponding to specific personality traits and life experiences.

Western astrologers create natal charts based on the exact time, date, and location of an individual's birth, analyzing the positions of the Sun, Moon, and planets and aspects.

Western Astrology relies heavily on natal charts, houses, and aspects, while Vedic Astrology incorporates lunar mansions and planetary periods to provide insights. Archaic Arkana Astrology employs a more intuitive and esoteric approach, often using symbols, archetypes and old style calculations.

Vedic Astrology:

Vedic astrology is the traditional Hindu system of astrology rooted in the ancient Indian scriptures (Vedas). The objective is to understand karmic patterns, influences of the cosmos, celestial bodies and timing of events to support guidance and personal growth.

The differences of these Astrology techniques:

Archaic Arkana Astrology, Western Astrology, and Eastern Vedic Astrology reflect the diverse ways in which humans seek to understand the cosmos and their place within the world. Each approach offers insights and wisdom through psychological explorations, karmic understanding, or spiritual symbolism.

Western Astrology employs the tropical zodiac based on seasonal changes, while Vedic Astrology uses the sidereal zodiac based on the actual positions of stars and constellations. Archaic Arkana Astrology often integrates both seasonal and celestial influences. Western Astrology tends to emphasize psychological insights and personal growth, focusing on the individual's character and life experiences. Vedic Astrology, on the other hand, emphasizes karmic influences and the spiritual journey, offering guidance on life purpose. Archaic Arkana Astrology leans towards the symbolic and archetypal, exploring deeper spiritual connections and specific predictions.

18
Runes

Runes are characters made from stone, wood or metal. My daughter Cheyenne made me a set of them. They derive from Old Germanic alphabets around the 1st century AD. Each stone is guidance for an event, relationship or issue.

Runes are often linked in mythology to the god Odin, the legend says, he discovered the runes while hanging from the World Tree, Yggdrasil, for nine nights. This myth underscores the spiritual and mystical dimensions of runes, connecting them to knowledge, sacrifice, and enlightenment. Therefore he became the symbol of the hangman in the tarot. On the 9th day he had created the runes.

However, some believe the characters evolved from the Etruscan and Latin alphabets. But the first runic writings were found in Scandinavia in Denmark, Sweden and Norway.

The runic alphabet consists of 24 characters. It is known as the Futhark (named after the first six letters: F, U, Þ, A, R, K).

The alphabet underwent different forms and variations, such as the oldest version Futhark, the younger version Futhark (Vikings used it in Scandinavia), and the Anglo-Saxon Futhorc (modified for the Old English version).

Runes

Fehu (F): Symbolizing wealth and prosperity, it represents cattle and movable wealth. This rune embodies the idea of abundance and the flow of resources.

Uruz (U): Associated with strength and primal energy, Uruz represents the aurochs, a wild ox. It signifies physical power, health, and the potential for transformation.

Thurisaz (Þ): This rune represents the thorn and is connected to protection and conflict. It embodies both the destructive and protective powers of nature, often linked to the giant Thurses in mythology.

Ansuz (A): Associated with wisdom and communication, Ansuz represents the gods, particularly Odin, who is the god of knowledge and inspiration. This rune signifies the power of words and the importance of communication.

Raido (R): Symbolizing movement and journey, Raido represents travel, cycles, and the passage of time. It embodies the idea of progress and the journey of life.

Laguz (L): Associated with water, Laguz represents intuition, emotions, and the subconscious. It signifies the flow of life and the importance of connecting with one's inner self.

The oldest Futhark is the most widely recognized variant, consisting of 24 runes. The runes are not only letters; they have symbolic importance and were often used for divination.

These meanings were often accompanied by specific rituals or spells, as runes were believed to possess inherent magical properties. They were carved into wood, stone, or metal, and the act of inscribing runes was considered a powerful magical practice.

Runes held importance in Germanic culture. They were used for various purposes, including marking territory, commemorating the dead, and inscribing important events.

Runes were also used in divination practices, where practitioners would cast or draw runes. The process of divination using runes, known as runecasting. Casting the Runes to gain the meaning of the symbols by their positions.

The interest in runes began in the 19th and 20th centuries, along with neo-paganism and interest in ancient spiritual practices. Today, runes are often used as tools for divination, meditation, and personal empowerment. Many people create their own rune sets, imbue them with personal meanings, and use them to connect with their spirituality.

"Wisdom is welcome wherever it comes from": ᚾᛁᛋᛏᛟᛘ ᛁᛋ ᚹᛖᛚᚳᛟᛘ ᚹᚺᛖᚱᛖᚹᛖᚱ ᛁᛏ ᚳᛟᛘᛋ ᚠᚱᛟᛘ.

19

I Ching

I Ching (The Book of Changes): This ancient Chinese divination system uses a set of 64 hexagrams. To use the system of the I Ching you do so by tossing coins or yarrow sticks. Each hexagram corresponds to a situation and how to handle that situation. The I Ching advises on adaptability and making conscious change.

The I Ching is also known as the Book of Changes. It is one of the oldest and most revered texts in Chinese philosophy. It began in ancient China, around the Western Zhou period (approximately 1046–771 BCE),. Although it may extend even further into the Shang dynasty (circa 1600–1046 BCE) and possibly even earlier. The I Ching is not only a book of divination; it is rooted in philosophical perspectives. The I Ching became fundamental in differing schools of thought, including Confucianism and Daoism.

The Original I Ching was a collection of oracular expressions of nature and human experiences. But it evolved into a more structured system. Integrating hexagram, consisting of straight lines or split-in-two straight lines that represent different challenges and change.

The hexagrams are arranged in pairs representing Daoist concepts of opposition and balance. The interaction of yin/yang—the feminine/masculine, inactive/active—the guidance, and advice of the I Ching is a practical tool for self-reflection.

The clarification of an I Ching reading hinges on deeper understanding the hexagram's meaning. Each hexagram contains a primary awareness text, and a second text provides a deeper insight into the first text.

The I Ching encourages everyone to embrace their changes in balance and harmony. It emphasizes self-awareness, inner-reflection, and changes. The wisdom of the I Ching is to provide guidance. The teachings of the I Ching inspire everyone to navigate the difficulties of life with grace.

Your Notes:

20

Psychometry

Psychometry is touching an object and receiving the psychic emanations and impressions. You can use a photo or someone's personal item. Write down all your impressions or record them. This is fun to do with a friend, but you can do this by even taking a photo of a celebrity, sports star, politician or someone you don't know but can verify the results and ask mundane questions such as their birth month, day or year. If they have siblings, married, children, what city or region - they are born or grew up. And then you can check your information.

Clairangency and psychometry are both psychic abilities that involve the perception of information through touch, but they have distinct characteristics and applications.

Clairangency is the broader term that refers to the ability to gain insights or sensations through touch. This can involve sensing the emotions, health, or energy of people or objects simply by making contact with them. Clairangency is often associated with empathic abilities, where the individual can feel or intuitively understand the emotional or physical state of another person through tactile interaction. It emphasizes the connection between the psychic and the physical, allowing for a deeper understanding of interpersonal dynamics and energies.

Psychometry, on the other hand, is a specific form of clairangency that focuses on the ability to obtain information about an object's history or the people associated with it by touching or holding that object. Practitioners of psychometry believe that objects can retain the energy of their previous owners or experiences, and by touching them, they can access this stored information. Psychometry often involves retrieving detailed insights about past events, emotions, or experiences connected to the object, making it a more focused practice compared to the broader applications of clairangency.

While both clairangency and psychometry involve the acquisition of information through touch, clairangency encompasses a wider range of tactile intuitive abilities, including empathic sensing and energetic perception, whereas psychometry specifically relates to the reading of objects and their histories.

How to practice Psychometry:

Close your eyes and breath deeply a few times, with your eyes closed concentrate on your inner-connection. Feel your chakras and power centers tingling or being activated. Focus on an object or person.

Do you see an aura?

Connect to their solar plexus. You might begin to see movies of an object. It's history, feelings and their journeys of the object and it's owner. What kind of information are you getting. Write or record your experience.

21
Pendulum

Pendulum Divination: This technique if a form of dowsing, it involves using a pendulum. A necklace or object found on a chain or string to answer questions. The pendulum swings either from your higher self, your spirit guide or an entity.

It's best to say a protection prayer first.

When the pendulum swings in different directions based on your question. There is different ways the pendulum will swing when indicating "yes," "no," or "maybe." This method is often used for decision-making. You can also use it for locating lost objects.

The first time I saw the pendulum in action. I was in a San Francisco grocery store and a lady named Sonia Levy was using her pendulum over produce. And… she let me try.

The pendulum is a fascinating and fun tool mostly used for divination, dowsing, and spiritual practices. The use of pendulums started back when used with dowsing, or "water-witching," trying to locate sources of underground water, The practice started in ancient China and Egypt. And it is known early dowsers used forked sticks or rods before developing to the pendulum form.

Pendulums gained popularity in 19th Century Europe with psychics and mediums who communicated with the spirits and the spiritual realms. The occult and spiritualist movement was quite popular then. Pendulums became recognized for their ability to access intuitive knowledge and provide answers to questions. Plus its one of the easier divinations systems to learn. As with all divination, it's best to be thoughtful and use all knowledge wisely.

Whether the pendulum is viewed as a tool for answers from the subconscious mind or by benevolent spirits. Communicating wisely when using a pendulum can give you lots of great answers.

How to use a pendulum:

Choose a pendulum or pendant that resonates with you. Pendulums can be made from crystals (amethyst, quartz, or rose quartz, or any stones), wood, or metal attached to a string or chain.

Clear Your Mind: Before beginning, take a few moments to center yourself. Practice deep breathing or meditation to clear your mind of distractions and create a receptive state.

Hold the pendulum by the chain. Ask your question. Let the pendulum swing without obstruction. This is the meanings of the pendulum.

Yes: Swings clockwise, or circling to the right.

No: Swinging counterclockwise or circling to the left.

Maybe: Erratic movement or back and forth,

Unknown: no movement at all.

Ask Your Questions, try and be clear and don't ask questions over and over.

Record Your Findings: Keeping a pendulum journal can be helpful. Document your questions, the pendulum's responses, and any insights or observations you gain.

Say a protection prayer before you begin.

The pendulum is a versatile tool that can be used for divination, dowsing, and spiritual exploration. Whether viewed as a means of accessing subconscious knowledge or as a conduit for spiritual communication, the pendulum offers valuable insights and guidance. By understanding how to use the pendulum effectively and trusting your intuition, you can unlock its potential as a powerful tool for self-discovery and decision-making. With practice and dedication, and staying grounded, the pendulum can become an integral part of your spiritual journey.

Your Notes or Prayer:

22
Tea Leaf Reading

Tea Leaf Reading: The original name for tea leaf reading is known as Tasseography. This technique is about deciphering the patterns and shapes formed by tea leaves left at the bottom of a cup after drinking "loose tea". The reader breaks down what they are seeing in the cup. Which can represent different details of the querent's life, offering insights into their past, present, and future and/or there can be a specific question asked.

Tea leaf reading has roots that extend back to the ways of tasseography in the Middle East and Europe. It is presumed that tea leaf reading made a reappearance as a form of divination in the 17th century, when tea drinking became popularized in Europe.

The tradition is often linked to the practice of reading coffee grounds also, and even wine sediments. Both have a similar methodology. As fortune-telling gained popularity in Victorian England, tea reading became a favored parlor game.

How can I do a Tea Leaf Reading

Conducting tea leaf reading involves a few steps, selecting a loose tea, boiling water for the tea pot and letting some of the loose tea be in the cup in the pour. Here's a step-by-step guide:

Choosing a good tea: Loose-leaf black tea or herbal tea is recommended. Do not use tea bags.

While you are having tea or a tea party. Drink the tea. And as you drink your tea, focus on a question.

Swirl your Cup, if there is still a small amount of liquid in the cup, gently swirl it three times. Stop, and hand your cup to the reader.

Examine the Leaves: Once the leaves have settled, carefully observe the patterns formed at the bottom of the cup. Look for shapes, symbols, and images created by the tea leaves.

Your tea will have shapes, and patterns. It is usually a symbolic reading. You can use a dream book to help you decipher what shapes and patterns your seeing.

Journal your Readings: Keeping a tea leaf reading journal can be beneficial. Record your interpretations, the symbols observed, and any insights gained. Over time, you can track patterns and deepen your understanding of the practice and it's always fun to do with your friends.

Tea leaf reading is an ancient specialty that offers a distinctive way to gain insights. I also like to read Turkish Coffee too. By observing the patterns formed by the coffee or tea leaves are fun to explore a persons questions, challenges, and potential outcomes. It makes a tea party fun!

"Numerology is the key to the secrets of the universe." - Pythagoras

23

Numerology

Numerology is an ancient metaphysical science that assigns meaning to numbers and explores their significance in our lives. It is based on the belief that numbers have inherent vibrational frequencies that can influence our personality, experiences, and even the events that unfold in our lives. This practice has roots in various cultures, including ancient Egypt, Greece, and China, and has been used for centuries to gain insights into personal and universal truths.

At its core, numerology operates on the premise that everything in the universe is connected through numbers, and that these numbers can be interpreted to reveal deeper meanings. Here are some key concepts and meanings associated with numerology:

Life Path Number: One of the most significant numbers in numerology is the Life Path Number, which is derived from your birth date. This number reveals your life's purpose, challenges, and opportunities. It is calculated by adding the digits of your birth date together until you arrive at a single digit (1-9) or one of the master numbers (11, 22, 33).

Expression Number: Aka Destiny Number is the "full name given at birth" calculation. It reveals your natural talents and abilities. Each letter is a specific number (A=1, B=2, C=3, D=4, E=5, F=6, G=7, H=8, I=9, J=1, K=2, L=3, M=4, N=5, O=6, P=7, Q=8, R=9, S=1, T=2, U=3, V=4, W=5, X=6, Y=7, Z=8), and the numbers are derived similarly to the Life Path Number.

Soul Urge Number: This number is derived from the vowels in your full birth name It symbolizes your soul's Motivation and your effectiveness.

Personality Number: The Personality Number is calculated using the consonants in your name. It shows your outward personality.

Personal Year Number: This number provides clues you might encounter in a specific year. It is calculated by adding your birth month and day to the current year. Each personal year is linked with a specific resonance that effects your agreements and/or disagreements..

Master Numbers: master numbers (11, 22, and 33) carry higher spiritual importance. They may carry spiritual insights, and considerable influence in the world.

Karmic Debt Numbers: Such as 13, 14, 16, and 19, are often referred to as karmic debt numbers. Challenges and disagreements considered to be in this life or a past life and need to be worked on and overcome.

Numerology is a powerful tool for self-discovery.

Life Path Number:

1: Action and independence
2: Succcess and Security
3: Communication and self-expression
4: Home Life and Family
5: Creativity and Meetings
6: Service and Health
7: Family/Friends and Others
8: Changes and Sensitivity
9: Environment and humanitarianism
11: Intuition and insight
22: Mastery and building
33: Altruism and service

24
Crystal Ball

Crystal Ball Gazing: This is a form of scrying that specifically uses a crystal ball. The practitioner gazes into the ball, often entering a trance-like state, to receive visions or intuitive messages. The clarity and depth of the crystal can enhance the experience, allowing for profound insights and connections.

Scrying: Scrying involves gazing into a reflective surface, such as crystal balls, mirrors, or water, to receive visions or insights. Practitioners enter a meditative state, allowing their intuition to interpret images, symbols, or emotions that arise. This modality is often associated with deep introspection and spiritual connection. This practice has been used across various cultures and traditions, often associated with mysticism and the exploration of the unseen. Scrying can take many forms, including using crystal balls, mirrors, water, or even polished stones. Here, we will explore the history, methods, and techniques of scrying in depth, along with tips for effective practice. I have used this form of divination very successfully in solving missing person cases.

Scrying has a long and varied history, with roots in ancient civilizations such as the Egyptians, Greeks, and Romans. The practice has been documented in texts from various cultures, including the use of crystal balls in medieval Europe, water scrying in ancient China, and the use of mirrors by the Aztecs and Native Americans. In these traditions, scrying was often associated with prophecy, spiritual guidance, and communication with deities or spirits.

The underlying belief in scrying is that the reflective medium can act as a portal to the subconscious mind or the spiritual realm, allowing the practitioner to receive insights, visions, or messages that may not be available through ordinary perception. This practice has evolved over time, incorporating various techniques and tools, but the core intent remains the same: to seek knowledge and understanding beyond the physical world.

The first step in scrying is selecting a suitable tool. Different mediums can evoke different energies and responses, so it's essential to choose one that resonates with you. Here are some common tools used in scrying:

Crystal Ball: A polished crystal ball, typically made from quartz, is one of the most well-known scrying tools. Its smooth, transparent surface allows light to refract, creating an ethereal visual experience.

Mirror: A black mirror or a darkened glass surface can facilitate scrying by reflecting light and creating a void-like depth. Some practitioners prefer using a regular mirror, while others may choose specially designed scrying mirrors.

Water: A bowl of clear water can be used for scrying. The surface of the water acts as a reflective medium, where the practitioner can observe ripples, reflections, or even the depths of the water.

Polished Stones: Smooth, polished stones like obsidian or onyx can also be effective for scrying. Their reflective surfaces can yield visions or insights when gazed upon.

Smoke: Some practitioners use the smoke from incense or a candle as a medium. The swirling patterns can reveal images or symbols as they form and dissipate.

The Scrying Process

Say a prayer to get a calm state of mind.

Take Your Position: Sit comfortably in front of your chosen scrying tool. Whether this is a black shiny surface mirror, water, or a crystal ball. Ensure that you can see your reflection or the surface clearly. You might need to scry in a dark room with a candle.

Breathe and let go of any expectation. You may find it helpful to repeat your intention or mantra silently. As you relax into the experience, pay attention to any shapes, images, symbols, wispy unclear images or feelings.. These come in the form of visions and colors.. be receptive as it might take a moment to be in the experience.

At the closing, express thanks and gratitude, visualize closing the energy you opened.

Note: Scrying can take time to develop. Don't be disheartened if you don't receive clear messages right away. Keep practicing.

Scrying is a powerful divination tool that offers profound insights and connections to the spiritual realm. By choosing a suitable medium, preparing your environment, and engaging in the practice with intention and openness, you can explore the depths of your consciousness and uncover hidden knowledge.

Your Notes:

25
Mediumship

Mediumship: People who become channels, I bet never thought they'd be the ones who speak to the dead. It's not like it's a comfortable vocation. Psychics are usually using some type of "clairs" or ESP. When becoming a channeler and medium, you are dealing with the other side. Spirits who have come to speak or communicate, usually they are just as anxious to speak to their loved ones and the loved ones are to speak to them.

How do I talk to spirits? I don't recommend saying, "Anyone come in!" That is asking for ghosts and accident victims to come and speak to you or through you... not a good idea. They usually are beings confused about themselves. They're only there for you to help them and you might not yet have the tools or know-how on where to start. Other than asking them to go to the light. You want great advice to messages from your relatives and spirit guides.

I recommend a guided meditation to "automatic writing" as a first step for becoming a medium and then you can change to allowing your voice to be used. But still it's tricky and you should be guided or do lots of research.

Mediumship is something most everyone wants to experience in their life. We all have to face death with people we love. It's not easy to connect the real world to the spiritual world. But some people are really gifted at it. Every experience with a medium is a journey of understanding, communication, and ultimately, healing. But the process involves more than communication, you have to ready yourself with the deceased entities that are often misunderstood or can't get their message clearly across the barrier.

I would refrain from any mind altering substances or alcohol. Be in a calm, quiet space allowing fro create the connection. Guided meditation is helpful, to help ground and center everyones energy creating a more receptive experience. You can also say a prayer of protection, there are a few later in this book to help you feel even more relaxed and attuned.

Once you feel inclined you can experiment with automatic writing. This is easiest to experience through a guided meditation.

When you feel ready to progress beyond automatic writing, you can begin to practice using your voice to channel. You will be looking for clear signs and dialogue. If there is any disrespectful or distressed messages. You should gently tell them to "go to the light". Remind yourself who you have chosen to talk to; they might want to express some of their confusion or disappointments.

It is important to remember that not all spirits and entities, or loved ones are aware of their present state, and some may need your guidance on directing them to go to the light and to explain your point of view what has happened to them and that they have passed from the earth. Be understanding and compassionate. Delegate your sentinels and the guides to help them to the light.

Becoming a channel/medium is one of practice. With guided meditations to practice with, you can, slowly expand and go toward automatic writing and then vocal communication. I would tape these sessions and have someone take notes.

26
Abenda, Tara's Spirit Guide

I'm giving you the internet's version of Abenda.

Abenda, as described in the teachings of Tara Sutphen, is a spirit guide who embodies wisdom, support, and a deep connection to the spiritual realms. Tara Sutphen, a prominent author, psychic, and spiritual teacher, introduces Abenda as a powerful figure who assists individuals on their journey towards enlightenment and self-discovery.

Abenda is portrayed as a benevolent and nurturing spirit guide who offers guidance, healing, and insight. Through Tara Sutphen's work, Abenda is often depicted as embodying qualities of compassion and understanding, serving as a bridge between the physical and spiritual worlds. Abenda is believed to possess a wealth of knowledge regarding both the earthly experience and the greater cosmic reality, making this guide particularly valuable for those seeking deeper truths about their existence.

Abenda's presence is often described as warm and enveloping, evoking feelings of safety and reassurance. Those who connect with Abenda report sensations of calmness and clarity, as if a gentle light is illuminating their path. This spirit guide is also associated with vibrant colors and swirling energies, symbolizing the dynamic nature of spiritual growth and transformation.

Abenda is characterized by an ethereal quality, often depicted with flowing garments and an aura that radiates peace and enlightenment. This visual representation serves to remind seekers of the beauty and grace that exists beyond the physical realm, encouraging them to embrace their own spiritual journey.

In Tara Sutphen's teachings, Abenda plays a crucial role in helping individuals unlock their potential and navigate life's challenges. This spirit guide is said to assist in various areas, including personal development, psychic enhancement, and healing practices. Those who seek Abenda's guidance may find themselves receiving intuitive insights, visions, or messages that provide clarity and direction.

Abenda encourages individuals to trust their intuition, reminding them that they hold the keys to their own empowerment. Through practices such as meditation or trance work, seekers can deepen their connection with Abenda, allowing for a more profound understanding of their life purpose and spiritual mission.

Abenda, as a spirit guide in Tara Sutphen's teachings, represents a source of strength, wisdom, and inspiration. This ethereal presence invites individuals to explore their inner landscapes and embrace spiritual growth. By fostering a connection with Abenda, seekers are encouraged to tap into their innate psychic abilities and navigate their journeys with confidence and clarity. Abenda serves as a reminder that the spiritual realm is always accessible, offering support and guidance to those who seek it.

There are books I've used Automatic writing with Abenda. Blame it on your Past Lives, The Abenda Chronicles, Abenda Writings, Soul Agreements, and Soul Writers. I also have an mp3 called Abenda Link for anyone who wants to try and automatic write with her.

Website - moonsorce .com
Store product page
abenda-link-automatic-writing-meditation

27

Automatic Writing

Communications began in 1982 with Automatic Writing, I primarily wrote about family and friends. All of whom encouraged me to keep at it, because the predictions turned out to be so accurate. I also began writing Numerology, Astrology, Handwriting Analysis articles for international magazines and popular publications, that's when my office manager suggested; I start writing "Cause & Effect" where People could send me questions about their problems and my Spirit Guide Abenda would choose the letters she felt would relate to many readers.

To receive the communications, I would go into a theta-level altered state, and Abenda would find someone on the other side that knows the letter writer, their spirit guide or a loving entity who is aware of the problem. Under my spirit guide's carefully orchestrated conditions, this soul controls my hand and the response was received via automatic writing.

MY TECHNIQUE: Upon attaining a self-induced theta state, I visualize myself in the center of a Celtic Druid circle. I feel the grass beneath my bare feet and I look upon the stone altar. I place a symbolic gift upon the altar (flowers, stones or feathers as an example) and I make a blessing for my earth life. Then I leave the circle feeling the earth and grass and feel myself running until I am flying out of earth's atmosphere. In time, I come to a white fog where I find stairs ascending up into the mist. The stairs are ancient, gray and worn. I reach out and touch the surface. Often I find flowers by the stairs. They've been left by my deceased Grandmother Gwendolyn, who is waiting at this level for her children to cross over.

Focusing my senses, I feel myself walking up the stairs, going higher and higher, until I come to a landing where Abenda awaits in the doorway to my "temple room."

Abenda and I hug upon meeting and then enter the room, which is furnished with unusual furniture, which I'm told is Persian. Yellow Chinese silk pillows abound and East Indian statuary accents the decor. In my earthly reality, I love Native American, Western and Spanish decor, but I am very comfortable here and can see, touch, smell the room. At this point, I feel an almost complete transference of energy. My physical body is numb and I no longer hear or see what is going on in my real life.

My temple-room time becomes my reality while I am there. I scrunch pillows to relax on the couch, while conversing with Abenda. Over the years, she's learned to joke and play with me. That took awhile, because she perceives our association as a working relationship, and she wants to keep the energy between us clear and precise. We get into intense conversations and we can even have arguments. Some of the disagreements relate to work versus play. Abenda doesn't live an earth life. She died brutally in her last incarnation and wants no association with our physical world other than to help me (and others) through our earthly trials and tribulations.

When I'm channeling for an individual who has written me about their problem, I physically hold their letter or another touchstone, such as a lock of hair or photograph. In trance, I visualize myself strolling out the back door of my temple room and going to a glass teahouse. Here, in this separate environment, Abenda calls in the letter-writer's spirit guide or someone on the other side who loves them through a past-life connection.

I perceive this soul, who has come to write through me, just as if they were actually sitting beside me here on earth. Usually, they come to communicate wearing what they wore in the past life they shared with the letter-writer. If they were shy and demure in a past life, they will appear the same today. A flamboyant man from a 1700s incarnation will still be showy when he walks into the teahouse to communicate.

Abenda has to provide an "okay" for an entity to write through my hand. Anyone from a lower vibration is not allowed contact. My spirit guide also stresses that a language other than English can be translated, but not written. If they have difficulty writing legibly, they can allow me to use my own handwriting.

Sometimes I feel like a spiritual phone connection. I realize my abilities go far beyond those normally expressed through this medium. Although, really anyone willing to practice can develop the ability to do automatic writing. I hold and prove this when teaching my Sedona Psychic Seminars, and I get a lot of feedback for those using my "Automatic Writing" MP3.

28
White Light Protection

Is it dangerous to explore your higher self, super consciousness, the other side, or the great universe? It's not harmful, unless you create it that way. If you are afraid of the dark, you may make others afraid with what you say. When giving advice, it should be always upbeat. Try to help yourself or someone else create solutions.

White Light Prayer

Open your hands to receive, as the light of the stars cascade down upon you.

Breathing deeply and relaxing, just, really relax. Allow the quietness of spirit and the God light to come over you. You are feeling so relaxed and so at ease and allowing your

body and mind to relax and rest. All that
lovely oxygen is filling your body and mind,
as the light expands and intensifies. You
experience the light. You become the light.
You emanate the light and invoke the blessing
of the sorce of the light.

You are protected for all things. Seen and
Unnseen, All forces and all elements.

Bless your Family and Friends. Bless your
Sage Wisdom and the Intuition now open in
all chakras.

You have balance and harmony. healing and
protection, solace and wisdom, for every level
of my spirit, body and mind.

Casting this protection deep within your
cellular memory and throughout your akashic
records. May you always be safe, in all ways.

Asking God and the sorce of the light now
enter your heart and with your extended
hands, you now bring them to your heart. To
Be Blessed, beyond measure…

We ask it, We beseech it, We mark it, and so it is…

You can say Amen or Aho, or express Gratitude in some way.

Your Notes or Prayer:

Follow your dreams, transform your life, take the path that leads to God. Perform your miracles. Cure. Make prophecies. Listen to your guardian angel. Transform yourself. Be a warrior, and be happy, as you wage the good fight. Take risks - Paulo Coelho

29
Prayers with Tara & Amy

Sometimes I end my private sessions with a prayer I create on the spot, tailored specifically for my client. My sister, Amy had just finished her second round of chemo for stage 4 cancer. So I asked if I could pray with her. Amy said, she'd recount the experience for you all.

Amy: Tara and I started praying together in May of 2020. We had the opportunity to take a beautiful trip together to the Puget Sound in Washington at that time. My niece and Tara's daughter, Cheyenne, was moving back to Los Angeles and we were there to help move her.

The town where we were staying was like an enchanted forest. We would walk to town everyday, or sometimes twice a day to get a tea, or visit the very few shops that were open during that covid time. Of course, during our walks we would discuss our own lives. My health had been on the mend from cancer again and it was time for my life to move back on track.

Tara suggested we pray. We found a beautiful bench on our trail and started our prayer. Tara told me, "we are going to call in our Sentinels." She explained, we were going to pray and ask ArchAngel Sentinels with clear intention, and ask for "what you really want". I knew I wanted a new job. I was working as a bartender at that time and I really wanted to move into a new direction.

To complicate things, most of the country was laid off due to Covid. Tara said "That doesn't matter. We ask our Sentinels with clear intention and they will lead us in the right direction." We meditated onto the cloud elevated plane, and I met with our Sentinels. I told them I wanted an office job, with good hours, good pay and a good company. I had years of experience in sales and construction, so I wanted something that was right along those lines.

Three weeks later, when I was back at home, I received a call from one of my daughter's friend's Mom. She is a General Manager at a local commercial cabinet shop. They were looking for a new administrative assistant, as the one they currently had was getting married and leaving the company. She asked me if I wanted to interview for the position.

I started off part time, which allowed me to continue to heal. As the world came back from covid, our shop became busier and busier. Five and a half years later, I'm now one of their Project Managers and the Office Manager.

Since then, Tara and I have prayed many more times. Each time it feels like magic. It's not just about asking for blessings, it feels like a direct divine line. A couple of years ago we were on the phone praying. We live a couple hundred miles away from each other, and talk when we can. But this night, it was really special. We were on our elevated cloud plane, and while we were there. I noticed there were some stone steps and a door. I asked Tara if she saw the door and the steps. She asked me, "what do they look like?"

I told her they were worn, stone steps. She says, "Those are steps to my temple room on the other side with my Spirit Guide, Abenda. I tell Tara, they want us to go into the room."

We walk in and they motion us to continue. I tell Tara, "They want us to go to Jess' temple room." Tara says, "Jess' temple room is connected to mine." Of course they were referring to Jess Stearn, our beloved family friend that had passed years before. When we arrived into the room, we were greeted by Jess, Patrick Smith, and our great grandmother Anna Cannon.

We gathered around Jess's table and all 3 of them gave us our special blessings and messages. Our grandmother Anna walked us out and as we walked out, we passed through Tara's garden. Grandma gave us flowers and we were able to say goodbye. It was just a magical experience, being beckoned on and seeing our friends and family. And even though Tara and I were hundreds of miles apart, we were able to experience it together.

As time has progressed, my connection to my Sentinels has grown very strong. Since that first time connecting with them in the Washington woods. Sometimes when someone is in trouble, I've asked them to go to the aid of family and friends when they need extra support. I call them in and Ask them to fly.

Your Prayer:

"First, have a definite, clear practical ideal; a goal, an objective. Second, have the necessary means to achieve your ends; wisdom, money, materials, and methods. Third, adjust all your means to that end."

-Aristotle

30
Your Thoughts Become Your Reality

I like to explore why the theory of creating intention can work, and how our thoughts become reality. There is a connection with our thoughts, feelings and behavior on what we can and cannot do. We can limit our potential by having inaccurate interpretations about ourselves. What labels have you placed on yourself. What are you thinking you can't do. Where are you placing a hold on your livelihood and why. What is the struggle. Where is the block. Whats holding up progress.

We can clearly see others flaws. Why is it we can't always see our own inadequacies. All adeptness is a step by step process. We witness others step into situations and events they know nothing about or where they are going to be fooled. You can view when others are doing the wrong thing at a mistaken time and learning the hard way. But it isn't about someone else, it's about you. You wouldn't touch a hot stove or stand in a swarm of bee's. We're in many of these allegorical scenarios every week, but we convince ourselves we're doing what is right instead of flow into a peaceful and productive lifestyle.

The idea that "your thoughts become your reality" is a powerful and transformative concept that suggests our mental and emotional states shape our experiences and perceptions of the world. This principle is deeply rooted in various philosophical, psychological, and spiritual traditions, emphasizing the profound interplay between thoughts, beliefs, and the material world. By understanding and harnessing this connection, individuals can actively create the reality they desire, leading to personal empowerment and fulfillment.

At the core of this idea is the understanding that thoughts are not merely fleeting mental events; they are energetic vibrations that influence our emotions, behaviors, and ultimately, our realities. Every thought carries a frequency that resonates with the universe, attracting similar energies and experiences into our lives. This phenomenon aligns with the principles of quantum physics, which suggests that consciousness plays a role in shaping reality. When we focus on positive, constructive thoughts, we align ourselves with energies that foster growth, opportunity, and abundance.

Conversely, negative thoughts can trap us in cycles of doubt, fear, and limitation. When we dwell on pessimistic beliefs or self-sabotaging thoughts, we inadvertently create barriers that hinder our progress and manifest undesirable circumstances. This dynamic highlights the importance of cultivating a positive mindset, as our internal dialogue directly impacts our external experiences.

Our beliefs serve as the foundation for our thoughts. They shape how we interpret our experiences and influence our responses to challenges. When we hold empowering beliefs, such as "I am capable of achieving my goals," we cultivate a mindset that is conducive to success. This belief system fuels our motivation, resilience, and determination, enabling us to take action toward our aspirations.

On the other hand, limiting beliefs—such as "I am not good enough" or "I will never succeed"—can create a self-fulfilling prophecy. These beliefs distort our perceptions, leading us to overlook opportunities and potential. By identifying and challenging these limiting beliefs, we can reframe our mindset and open ourselves to new possibilities.

One practical application of the idea that "your thoughts become your reality" is the use of visualization and affirmations.

Visualization involves mentally picturing desired outcomes, engaging the senses to create a vivid experience in the mind. This practice can enhance motivation, clarify goals, and reinforce positive beliefs. When we visualize success, we align our subconscious mind with our conscious desires, creating a powerful synergy that propels us toward our goals.

Affirmations are positive statements that reinforce desired beliefs and outcomes. By regularly repeating affirmations, we can reprogram our subconscious mind, replacing negative thought patterns with empowering ones. This practice serves to strengthen our resolve and cultivate a great mindset.

Being mindful of our thoughts is crucial for harnessing their power effectively. Mindfulness involves observing our thoughts without judgment, allowing us to recognize patterns and triggers. By cultivating awareness, we can identify negative thought patterns and consciously redirect our focus toward more constructive and positive thoughts.

Practices such as meditation, journaling, and deep breathing can enhance mindfulness, helping us cultivate a greater sense of control over our thoughts and emotions. When we learn to respond to our thoughts with awareness and intention, we can create a more favorable reality.

The notion that "your thoughts become your reality" underscores the profound connection between our inner world and the external experiences we encounter. By recognizing the power of our thoughts, beliefs, and perceptions, we can actively shape our realities and cultivate a life that reflects our true desires and potential. Embracing practices such as visualization, affirmations, and mindfulness empowers us to take charge of our thoughts, transforming them into catalysts for positive change and fulfillment.

In a world where we often feel powerless, this principle serves as a reminder that we hold the keys to our own realities, and by nurturing a positive mindset, we can unlock the doors to our dreams.

Your Notes and Dreams:

31

Life Lesson: Get Yourself On Track

Take a few minutes every day to meditate and connect to the divine. Expand your consciousness and your spiritual essence. To reconnect to your spiritual you is "your real job". Your soul will surpass your earth life. It's time to remember you are perfect in the eyes of God. You know you're connected to the planet with your feet firmly placed underneath you. Your life may be full of trials and troubles but the solutions will present themselves easily. Are you tuning into your inner sanctum or tuning out.

Where is the balance. As earthlings we are all different, but there is:

"A General Human Guideline"
Awake – sun up, Sleep – sun down, drink clean water, eat greens, fruit and protein as you truly are what you eat. Waste not and want not. Kindness will get you everywhere… kindness is not a weakness. Work diligently and smart. Choose or be chosen, develop skills and master abilities. Time is your bounty and blessings. Love and Love More.

PHYSICAL:

Health and the way we treat our cleanliness, posture, and overall treat our bodies is a part of being balanced. Our body is the most precious gift we have and without it we can't exist. If we don't stay healthy we certainly can't enjoy all the other aspects of life.

MENTAL:

You want to exercise your mind to keep it working properly. Keep your cognitive abilities sharp. If you don't take care of your body it will deteriorate, and this can also be true of your mind.

EMOTIONAL:

Managing emotions is important. When engaging with ours and others feelings, it's best to work with intelligence. In this way we learn how to be fulfilled. Remember to resolve any hurt feelings, never be irrational. It's easy to forget how to manage our emotional world.

SOCIAL:

There is a certain amount of human socializing people need. We learn to treat humankind with courtesy and fairness when we are interacting with each other. Sometimes there are wonderful connections we naturally make. Camaraderie and joy can easily be attained. There are some people who don't like to interact with society, perhaps they are introverted or afraid. And how about when dissension or bad feelings come up, those need to be handled. Often a small shift of perception can change your viewpoint and lead you to a fortunate outcome. Generally there is a certain spacial sharing humans need.

FINANCES:

Whether you are working in a career or a job, it's important to bring value to yourself. We are all a part of a cycle of service to mankind. It's honorable to assist ourselves, family and friends. Money is an energetic transference. What you give, you get back in some way 100 times better. Learn what your skills are and practice being the best you can be.

SPIRITUAL:

The relationship you create between yourself and the universe. You can fight your life every day or you can come into resonance and be in reverence of all the opportunities and possibilities life has to offer you. If you begin to feel blessed, this will carry into your speaking ability, actions and into a better future.

Whatever the mind of man can conceive and believe, it can achieve."
-Napoleon Hill

32
Illusion -vs- Reality

It is through the nine senses that we are aware of the world around us, and believe that it is real. When we see the solid objects around us, and are aware of them, it is hard to deny the validity of what we see. Everything looks to exist, and therefore, we never stop to question this actuality.

Our mind receives information through the nine senses and accepts it as factual, without questioning. When we bump into a table or a wall and feel pain, it is difficult to say that we are imagining the discomfort. When we see the world around us, hear sounds, smell scents, or feel heat or coldness, we cannot deny that these are facts, and we therefore, accept these sense impressions as real.

Eastern philosophies say that the world is an illusion, Maya in Eastern terminology. Maya or Māyā (Sanskrit: māyā), means "illusion" and "magic". In an earlier older language, it implies miraculous power and wisdom.

- *Can we accept illusion when everything looks so real*
- *Do we look at the world as a product of the imagination*
- *Is reality just imagination and illusion*

We use the nine senses and the mind to be cognizant of the world. Something real always exists. It does not come and go. However, there are gaps, when for us, the external world does not endure, such as while we sleep or in deep meditation. This also happens when we are so busy that we are not conscious of what is going on around us.

After we wake up from sleep, or when we come out of deep meditation and return to ordinary consciousness, we feel that there was a gap in our consciousness, in which the outside world hardly existed for us. There was no world for us at that time. I am not saying that the world ceased to exist at these moments, it came to a standstill for us, for our consciousness and awareness of it.

The world exists for us only when the nine senses and mind are directed towards it, and fades away for us when we silence the senses and the mind. During deep sleep, we do not experience the world, because our nine senses are not active. Can you prove the reality of the world while you are deeply asleep. After you wake up from sleep, other people might tell you that the world existed while you slept, but can you prove that these people prevailed while you were asleep.
After waking up, we may believe in the reality of the world. However, the fact is that during sleep the world was non-existent. During sleep, dreams seem very real, but upon awakening, we realize that they were just dreams. It could be the same with this world we call reality.

This leads back to our question, is the world illusion or reality. Reflecting on this concept can expand insight and understanding. Every person interprets experiences, details, words, and other people's behavior in a different ways. According to our subconscious programming and education.

No one's world is like another

Your Notes:

33
Psychic Danger Signs

I looked up at the sky and thought to myself; there is the line clouds staring at me. They were not chem trails, they were actual line clouds. The type my dearest deceased friend Treesa use to excitedly tell me about and read as an "I Ching" message. So I got off the freeway and I put the "I Ching" message in my iPhone notes to check when I got home. It was January 6th, 2025 and it had been a calm day. Upon sitting down at home and opening the I Ching book: My eye's popped open as I read the message:
"Danger".

The meaning: It is careless to goad danger but critical not to shrink from it. When dangerous conditions present themselves, you must remain calm in chaos. Gather your courage. Stay Brave, Alert and Focused.

First special message: Wait and let things reveal themselves. Strive for clarity of mind. The way out of danger is blocked. There will be a time of disorder, all you can do is wait… keep persevering in high-minded conduct, you become a living example to your family and fellow man. Inspire others to create order, thus you and others will be protected.

I know better than to just wave this message away! I wondered Whoa, what is up!?" The next morning, I was getting ready to head to Pacific Palisades to do sessions with five attorneys. We had changed our schedule the month before because of the Franklin Fire in Malibu. And now we had another "RFW - Red Flag Warning". I got a text on my phone to stop forward progress toward the residence I was going to visit. A fire had broken out in the Palisades. Again this visual came up for me; my "inner sight" would see a front door, swinging open and I would walk in and a chair would be there with a printed throw over it and a lamp which was turned on, and then as I looked deeper into the room, it would be "only blackness". I saw this vision a few times when I thought of the destination, it would then fade into a nothingness. I would think, what is going on…

And yes… the house burnt down in the Palisades fire.

When do you take your psychic self seriously? I'm someone who has always seen/heard/felt intuitively. I experience and sees psychic symbols, which are images, signs, or even objects that hold a specific message. I would write many of my observations or hunches down when I first wanted to keep a track record. I still record much of what I interpret when I'm reading for others.

I consider the "I Ching" shamanic symbolism. The I Ching is, also known as the "Book of Changes" is an ancient Chinese divination system used for guidance and decision-making. It contains 64 hexagrams, which are six-line figures of yin/yang lines, and philosophical commentaries.

I wondered who would be giving me messages in the sky? Would Treesa be that powerful? Is it a message from God or the Angels? Definitely the cloud formations were a warning from some higher powers that be.

Many of us get these messages all the time, but we put them off as they don't fit our schedule or mindset. I teach psychic ability, just for times like this... many think its to be a psychic reader, but it's for everyone to open their mind to observe how we can be safe and head in the direction that serves our lives. Safety first, health second, success third, love fourth, and fun and games fifth.

How do you recognize "psychic danger" signs? You could have a dream, or even a day-dream. You can hear something and it's repeated. You can have the inner-knowing, or you can feel it deeply in your gut. Is your mind awakened to these messages? It's much different than just being a fearful person or worrywart. You know when you are going toward "good energy". And it's best if you do mental conditioning and exercises to begin to see patterns or signs if you're curious or too worried..

Many people mix up reality and illusion in psychic predictions. And this is where people are leery of learning simple techniques. The reality is as humans we are traveling on planet earth which is jettisoning approximately 65,000 mph through space. As a species, we are all afraid of change. Gravity keeps us rooted onto the planet, it is the reason we age… maybe it's a blessing that it is much slower than it could be. Our senses are dimmed. Therefore our antenna isn't as sharp as it could be. We have to study things, our natural radiance is squashed due to the gravity pull. As souls, we don't remember where we came from or where we'll go when we die. It could be a dilemma, but it really isn't. So many people clip-clop through life without a care of themselves or others and still make it to a departure date. But wouldn't it be nicer if we individually released some of that gravity weighing us down and began an easier path of a good to great destiny. Tuning into our "tingler-senses".

When I had near-death experiences, I had to manage what all I was seeing, hearing and feeling. I found hypnosis and wrangled it in... I was a wide open vessel and found that largely others need to practice opening their senses once again. Usually people who are worrying a lot are empathetic but don't know where it comes from... could be a person next to you on the street, in a store, family or friends.

A few years ago, I heard a woman at my barn say "I'm going to die if I try to ride my horse bareback" (and at the time I felt inconvenienced and, why did I have to hear that! I could've come an hour earlier?) But then, I heard her say "die" again and then *again*. And I knew, I was the one who had to do something. So when she got on her horse, I held him at the reins on the "off side".

Thankfully, as the "near side" was a big wooden mounting platform and I would've been thrown into it. Within seconds, I was in the chest of her horse, as it was rearing. The horse was stumbling backwards.

Complete Chaos and out of control. I was still attached, in the air with this horse of course and the owner was thrown to the ground. And the horse was going to fall right on top of this woman, so I yanked him in the air as hard as I could, to fall the opposite way. The woman, was visibly shaken. She never said, Thank you, and she never did notice she was in danger that day.

Thankfully, my horses are lambs. But I work with them almost everyday I do horse therapy too. And all the horses I've used in horse therapy have really liked it. When I would show up, they would all beg to be chosen to work with me and the client.

We find ourselves in dilemmas each and every day. Driving. Crossing the street. Tripping over our own feet. Let's use our senses to make the right decisions in our lives.

So what incredible skill would you like to learn first? Tuning into your past, present, and/or future? Or becoming proficient in a clair, or all of them?

Clairvoyant - Clear sight and visions through their mind.

Clairsentient - Clear feeling and tuning in to feel your feelings.

Clairaudient - Clear hearing and audible messages from their higher self, your higher self, their spirit guides or angels.

Claircognizant - Clear knowing - gut feelings and inner and outer knowing.

Listen to yourself and others as they give the greatest clue on where you need to start developing instincts. Remarks such as "I hear ya", "yes, I see", "I know" or "ya know", "I feel for you" — Identifying in some way gives you clues on what is your and others' strongest clair.

And, if you are getting bad thoughts or feelings. What might it mean. And if you are worrying raise your vibration and you can say some prayers.

And this is the bottom line: Using your psychic ability is to gain clear and practical advice, not create instability or chaos. It is to stabilize your heart and mind.

We are given gifts to help us make the right choices in our lives and not wrong turns. Psychic ability is all about you and becoming your best self, and your healthy you.

Your Notes:

"Folks are usually about as happy as they make their minds up to be." - Abraham Lincoln

34
Private Sessions

Psychic Reading
Hypnotherapy
Therapy
Couples Therapy
Horse Therapy
Horse Group Therapy
Past Life Regression
House Clearing

35
Shamanic Horse Therapy

Horse therapy is effective in processing emotions and forming bonds of allowing trust and risk in our lives. If you've been depressed, anxious, lost, or unsettled. This may be the therapy for you. You will be working with a gentle show horse on the ground without riding. There are also riding lessons available, but not in the Horse Therapy Session.

Horse therapy is an easy way to get in touch with thoughts and feelings. Many people struggle with depression, loneliness, and trauma. Re-learning ways to cope and soothe ourselves might be reaching out to a big, warm, fuzzy animal with an amazing big heart and who is non-judgmental. They don't care about the past; they live in the present and forward motion. Horses are not into blame, denial, or drama. They want to enjoy you. And since their lives are as domesticated caged animals, they want to find fulfillment in their time with us as we do with them. Truly unconditional, horses thrive when they emotionally facilitate us to become better humans.

Horses are unique in how they sense our moods and emotions and react accordingly. Whether you are happy or sad, they will try and soothe you or stay quiet and hold sacred space for you. Horses have a similar dynamic of shutting down communication when they feel ignored, misunderstood, and isolated. They are social animals, and they may not speak English, but they are excellent communicators. You can hold fast to your old communication methods or develop new ones.

Horses are large animals and can bring a variety of emotions out of you. One of them is fear, and another is being liked. This is their biggest fear, too. You begin a process of bonding instead of escapism. They do not lie or manipulate, they do not judge or blame. They are healers.

The horse-human heart connection is a profound and multifaceted relationship that transcends mere companionship or utility. This bond is rooted in shared experiences, emotional resonance, and an innate understanding between species. As highly social and intuitive animals, horses have been companions to humans for thousands of years, and the connection between them is characterized by empathy, trust, and mutual respect.

Horses are remarkable creatures known for their sensitivity to human emotions and their ability to respond to subtle cues. This sensitivity allows them to form deep connections with humans, often facilitating a unique bond that goes beyond language. The horse-human heart connection is an intricate interplay of emotional awareness, physiological responses, and psychological engagement, creating a relationship that can be both healing and empathy.

At the core of the horse-human heart connection lies emotional resonance. Horses are prey animals, and as such, they possess a heightened awareness of their environment and the emotional states of those around them. They can sense fear, anxiety, joy, and calmness in humans, responding in ways that reflect those emotions. This ability fosters a deep empathetic connection, where both parties can feel understood and validated.

When a human approaches a horse with fear or apprehension, the horse may display signs of anxiety or agitation, mirroring the human's emotional state. Conversely, when a human is calm and centered, the horse often reflects that peace, allowing the bond to deepen. This emotional exchange creates a safe space for individuals to explore their feelings and develop greater self-awareness, as horses provide immediate feedback on their emotional states.

Research has shown that the heart plays a crucial role in the horse-human connection. The heart emits a powerful electromagnetic field, which can be detected several feet away from the body. This field is influenced by the emotional states of both the horse and the human, creating an energetic interplay that enhances the connection between them.

Studies humans and horses heart rhythms synchronize, creating a state of coherence. This synchronization promotes feelings of connection, well-being, and harmony, enhancing the bond between the two beings. In this way, the horse-human heart connection is not only emotional but also physiological, relying on the heart's intrinsic ability to influence and respond to the emotional landscape of both species.

The horse-human heart connection offers numerous therapeutic benefits, making it an essential component of equine-assisted therapies. These benefits include:

Emotional Healing: The non-judgmental presence of horses allows individuals to explore their emotions in a safe environment. This can lead to healing from past trauma, anxiety, and depression.

Stress Reduction: Interacting with horses has been shown to lower cortisol levels and reduce stress, promoting relaxation and emotional balance.

Improved Communication Skills: Working with horses requires clear communication and body language, helping individuals develop better interpersonal skills and emotional intelligence.

Enhanced Self-Esteem and Confidence: Building a relationship with a horse fosters a sense of accomplishment and self-worth, as individuals learn to care for and connect with these powerful animals.

Mindfulness and Presence: The need to be fully present when interacting with horses encourages mindfulness, helping individuals cultivate a deeper awareness of their thoughts and emotions.

The horse-human heart connection is a rich tapestry of emotional, physiological, and psychological elements that fosters deep bonds between these two species. Through empathy, synchronization of heart rhythms, and shared experiences, horses provide unique opportunities for healing, growth, and self-discovery. This connection reminds us of the profound impact that animals can have on our emotional well-being, encouraging us to explore the depths of our own hearts while fostering a mutual understanding that transcends words.

Shamanic horse therapy is an innovative and holistic healing practice that combines the ancient wisdom of shamanism with the therapeutic benefits of working with horses. This approach leverages the natural instincts and intuitive capabilities of horses, providing a unique environment for personal growth, emotional healing, and spiritual development. Rooted in both equine therapy and shamanic traditions, this practice fosters a deep connection between humans and horses, facilitating profound transformations in individuals seeking healing and self-discovery.

Shamanism is an ancient spiritual practice found in various cultures worldwide, where shamans act as intermediaries between the physical world and the spiritual realm. They use rituals, drumming, and altered states of consciousness to connect with spirit guides, ancestors, and the natural world to heal and provide guidance. Similarly, equine therapy is a form of experiential therapy that utilizes horses to promote emotional, psychological, and physical healing. It is based on the understanding that the presence of horses can evoke powerful emotional responses and foster trust, communication, and self-awareness.

When combined, shamanic horse therapy creates a synergistic effect, allowing individuals to access deeper layers of their psyche and connect with their spiritual selves through the guidance of horses. This practice emphasizes the importance of mindfulness, presence, and the healing power of nature.

The process of shamanic horse therapy typically involves several key components, each designed to facilitate healing and self-exploration:

Creating a Sacred Space: The therapy begins with the establishment of a safe and sacred environment. Practitioners may use rituals, such as smudging with sage or setting intentions, to create a space that is conducive to healing. This helps participants feel grounded and open to the experience.

Connecting with the Horse or Horses: Participants engage with horses in various ways, often beginning with simply being present with them. Horses are highly intuitive beings and can sense human emotions, providing immediate feedback. This connection allows individuals to explore their emotions, fears, and desires in a non-judgmental space.

Shamanic Journeying: Through guided visualization or drumming, practitioners may facilitate shamanic journeying, where participants enter altered states of consciousness to connect with their inner selves and spirit guides. This journey often leads to insights, healing messages, or guidance related to their personal challenges.

Equine Interaction: Activities may include grooming, leading, or riding horses, which promote trust, communication, and emotional expression. The horse's natural behaviors and responses help participants reflect on their own emotions and patterns, fostering personal growth and self-awareness.

Integration and Reflection: After the activities, participants are encouraged to reflect on their experiences, discussing insights gained during the session. This integration process is crucial for understanding how the lessons learned can be applied to everyday life.

The benefits of shamanic horse therapy are vast and multifaceted. Some of the key advantages include:

Emotional Healing: The non-verbal communication between horses and participants allows for the exploration and release of suppressed emotions, leading to emotional healing and resilience.

Increased Self-Awareness: Participants gain insights into their behaviors, thought patterns, and emotional responses, fostering greater self-awareness and personal growth.

Connection with Nature: The therapeutic environment encourages a deeper condition with nature, promoting relaxation and grounding.

Spiritual Development: The integration of shamanic practices allows individuals to connect with their spiritual selves, enhancing intuition and personal insight.

Building Trust and Communication Skills:
Working with horses cultivates trust, empathy, and effective communication skills, which can be transferred to human relationships.

Shamanic horse therapy is a powerful and transformative healing practice that combines the wisdom of shamanism with the therapeutic qualities of horses. By fostering deep connections with these intuitive beings, individuals can embark on a journey of self-discovery, emotional healing, and spiritual growth. This unique approach not only honors the ancient traditions of shamanism but also recognizes the profound impact that horses can have on our well-being, making it a valuable tool for those seeking holistic healing and personal transformation.

36
Tara Sutphen Seminars

Tara has been facilitating workshops and empowering people to deeply connect with their soul's calling, develop their psychic abilities, erase their deep-seated fears and blocks, help with health, manifest their soulmates, and much more for over 30 years.

The sharing that takes place in her workshops is transformational. Whether you are connecting with animals, other people, your mystic, guides, and masters, or your higher self, you will find yourself overwhelmed with happiness, deeply aware, and/or feeling your connections are finally crystal clear, honest, and true.

Book your spot in an upcoming seminar, for a private workshop with Tara, or to schedule a Psychic Party or request Tara to officiate a Ceremony.

Your Notes:

Your Notes:

Tara Sutphen CHt is an author, hypnotherapist, psychic, and spiritual teacher known for her work in the fields of metaphysics and personal development. She often focuses on topics such as intuition, healing, and self-discovery.

Sutphen has written several books and offers workshops and seminars aimed at helping individuals tap into their spiritual potential and enhance their intuitive abilities. If you have specific questions about her work or teachings, feel free to ask.

Your Notes:

On the Moonsorce website there are Automatic Writing MP3's

Automatic Writing
When you are in need of guidance, this gentle meditation helps you reach beyond the veil and allow the thoughts and love of the deceased to give you helpful and positive messages.

If you'd like to read a little more about Tara:

Aspiring Magazine Article

Aspiring Magazine March/April 2022

ASPIRING MAGAZINE

TARA SUTPHEN CHT FEATURE ARTICLE

I want to start out with where you were born, where you grew up. What was your life like?

I grew up in two states, Alaska and California. My mother, Marianne grew up in Anchorage, Alaska. She was born in a tent in Palmer and grew up on a homestead. When I was conceived, she was a nurse in Hollywood. She went back to Alaska to work in a Native Hospital for most of her pregnancy before moving to Seattle, Washington where I was born. Birth itself was a struggle for me. I immediately had to have an emergency surgery that lasted almost eight hours. The hospital Chaplin had little hope in my recovery. He read me my last rites and sent my mother home. It was my first near death experience. As a baby, I remembered everything. I could recount details of my everyday life with my parents and great-grandparents. There was a heightened awareness of how my family was feeling about things and how to act accordingly.

My father, Richard was born and raised in Santa Cruz, California. We moved between states because of his projects. He was an engineer, and I was born in Seattle because of his work on the Space Needle for the World Fair. My parents influence inspired my innovative work ethic and desire to help others. I was already considered a different child, spiritually aligned with people and things. My second near death experience was when I was eight years old. I was in a bicycle accident and began to hemorrhage. My father drove me to the hospital and the doctors wheeled me straight into emergency surgery. When I was moved from the gurney to the operating table, I took my last gasp and experienced my soul gravitating towards the light. This second NDE awakened a deeper connection to my intuition that would only grow stronger as I explored the intricacies of spiritual connection.

When I became a teenager people of a higher vibration would gravitate to my energy. Such as shamans, psychics and the masterful seers of the world. Wherever I was they would seek me and read me without payment or prompting. These spiritual guides were from Asia, the Philippines, Australia, Brazil, India, Native American Tribes, Russia, Africa and local. It was as though they were drawn to me from the light within us all, guiding us on our life paths. From birth I have been guided and tested in my ability to walk with my feet in both this reality and the one beyond the veil. My true purpose is to heal and secure the confidence of the mind, body, and spirit connection. The power of the mind has experiential potential. Our perspectives define the limits of our human experience. With practice and patience I believe everyone has the ability to expand their psychic awareness.

What drew you to Astrology?

I was 18 when I went to work on the Alaska pipeline, which is deep in the Arctic. Up in the vast frozen wasteland, I met a security guard for BP and an astrologer, Sharva Venta. His dad was a famous deceased Beatnik Krishna Venta, who was a big tadoo in Box Canyon back in the late 1950s. Sharva asked if I would like my astrology done. I didn't know what he meant really, as it was before all the computer technology. He wrote out my chart by hand, and it was about 50 pages of this small handwriting. It was inspirational and eye opening as it depicted the very essence of my character. After encountering Sharva Venta, I became fascinated with astrology and have studied it all these years. Mastering the mathematics and star blueprints that define the complexity of human personalities.

Who influenced you to go public with your work?

I had many teachers, although It wasn't until I moved from Anchorage, Alaska to Ojai, California at the age of twenty one, that I met my mentors and spiritual partner. I have a great deal of affection and gratitude to my dear friend, Jess Stearn. We met at Sarno"s restaurant in Hollywood. The owners Alberto and Savannah had this big table where they would sit 12 or 14 people, but it was bench style so you could get locked in the middle. Jess had been seated by me and we were "stuck". Alberto says, "tell something psychic to Tara". He took my hand and raised it to his forehead, he guessed the month I was born. I said "yes", he then did the same thing to the date of my birthday, I said "yes" and then he said the year. Right then and there I think we were sealed. But then he asked me, if I wanted to come to a seance' at his house that next week. For whatever reason, I declined and yet a few weeks later our paths crossed again at the same restaurant. He invited me to dinner in Malibu and our friendship bloomed. Jess

Stearn was a great author and became one of my dearest friends of my life.

In the beginning, I didn't know his books but he covered Eastern thought for the Western World. Primarily through one of his NY Bestsellers "Yoga, Youth & Reincarnation" (1965). Jess introduced me to Dick Sutphen, whom I married on Jess' deck in the early eighties. Jess and I were so divinely connected that later Dick and I had our daughter, Cheyenne on Jess's Birthday April 27th. Between those two men, psychic phenomena and hypnotherapy became my everyday life and obsession. I became a certified hypnotherapist and penned a column called "Cause & Effect" where I used automatic writing and my psychic ability to answer readers personal problems with supernatural solutions.

Did you have to go to college for that?

During my youth there wasn't metaphysical schools on the west coast as there are today. I went to traditional college for equine science. I've always had a soft spot for animals and believe we can connect with them by using concentrated energy and tone. I really wanted to be a veterinarian. I studied for three years at Equine Science School, but I had three kids to raise. I was trying to find balance with being a mother, running a non-profit organization and traveling to seminars on the weekend. So, I switched gears and attended Art school for another three plus years to give myself a creative outlet for the chaos of parenthood and psychic exploration.

I asked my husband if we could open a bookstore and I called it "Malibu Shaman" which is still in Malibu, California today owned and run by Dick's oldest son, Scott. I was able to order any book, I studied the Psychic Sciences: Automatic Writing, Hypnotism, Channeling, Sorcing, Palmistry, Psychometry, Handwriting Analysis, Esoteric Astrology, Shamanism, & Mysticism, etc. My dedication to metaphysics lead to teaching seminars all over the planet and away from merchant life.

Why were you nominated for Grammys

I was nominated for Grammy's when I began writing meditations and recording them. I was grouped with all the inspirational speakers and comedians where they give awards before the music awards. Looking back, it was a beautiful experience. It was fun to dress up and go to the Grammys to see if I was going to win or not. I was rather shy but had to be ready to accept an award, so I composed myself accordingly. I wore black velvet. and another year a long beautiful blue gown. There were pretty people everywhere, and amazingly dressed, certainly moments that I will never forget. I felt very honored to be nominated for my work.

How many books have you written?

I've written Five books and am currently writing my sixth book right now. The books I've written are Soul Writers, Blame It On Your Past Lives, Soul Agreements, Abenda Chronicles, and the Abenda Writings. Abenda is my spirit guide, I met her when I had my near death experiences. She said she'd work with me one day, but I didn't really know what she meant at the time. When I began the books, she would come through and give such great advice. If I wanted to know something about you, I would ask Abenda. I'd call to my guide and she'd converse with your spirit guide or someone who loves you very much and then they write through my hand. I did that for many years. People loved those letters. The book I'm writing now is a little different, I've taken people I know who have died and they are telling us what it is like on the other side.

What's something different you are doing in your industry?

I have a radio show and am doing Equine Therapy. The radio show is called "Transformations with Tara" you can hear me on iHeart and Spotify. I've been a radio host since 2008, and recommend it to anyone who wants to be a conscious voice in the world. My show is aired Friday mornings at nine a.m. Pacific time. We start out with a FB Live, I bring on special guests or my brother, Jason D.

McKean AKA Om Tarot Wizard as a co-host to discuss topics and phenomena. Jason is a wise wizard and spiritual teacher, he ran Dick and my company Valley of the Sun for thirty years, he has sold over a million copies of OM recordings throughout the world and written a successful book on Tarot you can find on Amazon called "Magic Channel Tarot Reading with the Tarot Wizard". He is a master of Tarot and does many classes including on-going teachings for Japan.

I conduct many seminars all over the globe and do in person or remote private sessions. I've led a variety of workshops on many metaphysical subjects and psychic development. Currently the most unusual class I am offering is therapy with horses for healing peoples inability to connect or bond due to traumatic experiences on their life path. They've been incredible appointments. I mostly lead these sessions in Los Angeles, but I'm always open to travel. I work with suggested imagery, shamanic techniques and visualization, I have 12 horses to choose from and they click in right away to the work. I show up and they can't wait to be chosen. I should say, most of the people who book the horse therapy appointments have never been around horses.

Any last minute words of encouragement?

The power of your mind is a fantastic tool and even more phenomenal when we learn some psychic abilities, meditation or visualizations to enhance our human experience. We all come up against problems, but there is always a way out. It's very important that we take steps in building a life that nurtures your mind, body and spirit. Environments and influences can always be changed with the right form of motivation and discipline. We create our reality, it's that simple.

Well, this has been wonderful and I can't wait to see you again!

Tara Sutphen lives in Los Angeles, California with her two Horses and two Dogs

the
Tara
Sutphen
Family

Tara
Hunter & Everest
Alex & Cheyenne
Will & Karissa
Lirica & Dakar
Sophia & Ghost

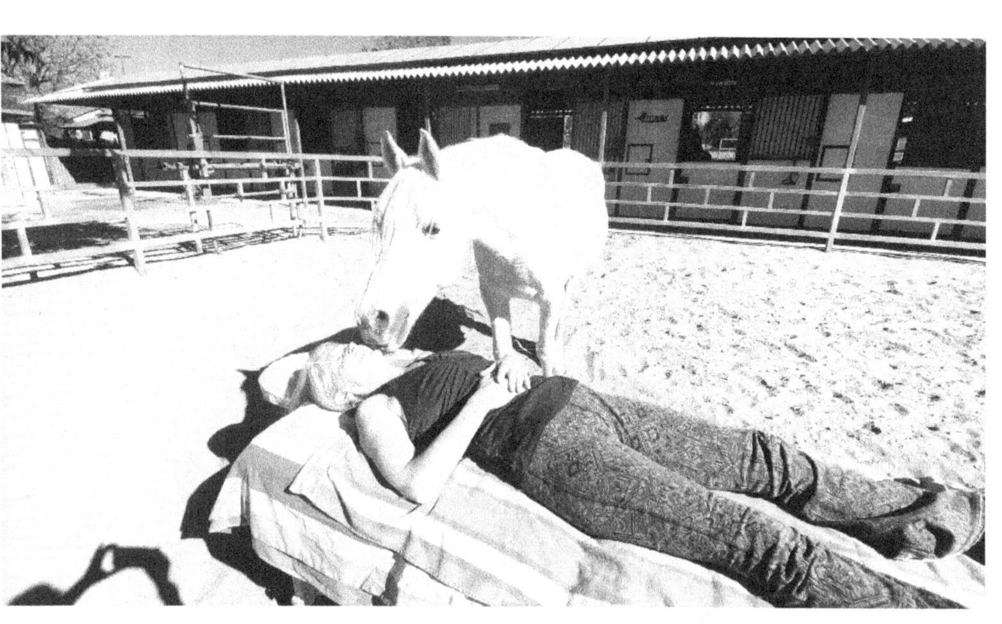

I can't wait to hear your progress on your psychic skills!